The Other designs.
Historical authenticity as artistic project

Athens/Zürich 2014

Content

p. 5	Heiko Schmid & Kostis Stafylakis: Introduction
p. 9 - 15	Heiko Schmid: Notes on authenticity. The art of establishing historic narratives.
p. 19 - 25	Robin Klimecki: Reflections on the Greek Sovereign Debt Crisis and the Condition of the "Indebted Man".
p. 29 - 33	Vassilis Vlastaras: "Dekavala's plan on upgrading and rethinking of Athens *Self-portrait V*"
p. 35 - 41	Natasa Biza: A Plan for Planting
p. 43 - 49	Romy Rüegger: Rerouted and Disordered: On Backgrounds and Background Listening - a Narrative Investigation
p. 51 - 55	Zafos Xagoraris: Minor Alterations of Legal Texts or other Regulations
p. 59 - 64	Elpida Rikou & Eleana Yalouri: Of Roots and Cultures.
p. 69 - 74	Sofia Bempeza: Evacuating the Political. New Greek Patriotism in the context of People's Movements.
p. 79 - 87	Kostis Stafylakis: The specter of historical authenticity in today's palingenetic radicalism and the dilemmas of radical art.

All Photos by Roland Regner (except p. 29 - 55)

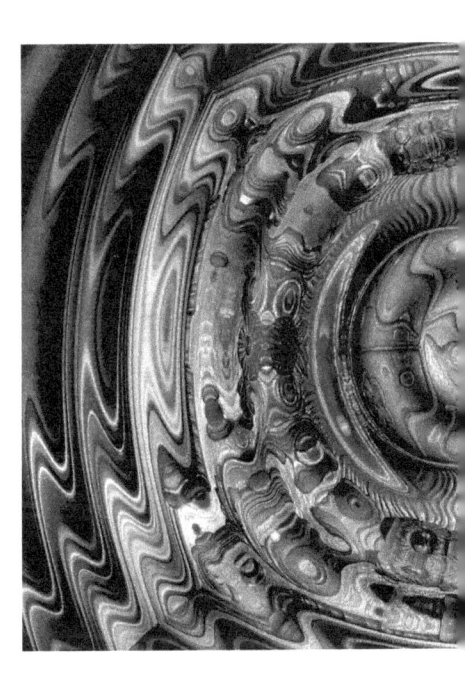

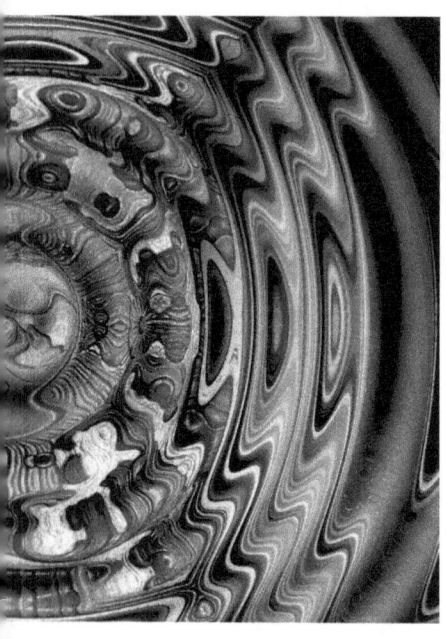

"All countries are burdened by their history, but the past weighs particularly heavily on Greece." This sentence opens up historian Richard Clogg's book *A concise history of Greece*. And Clogg, at the beginning of his book further speaks of a "burden of antiquity" Greece is carrying, but leaves no suggestion of how history can develop "weight" at all.

To explain this "burden" all countries have in regard to their past, and using Greece as an example, one has to explore various historical layers. A starting point could be the initial unveiling by central-European archaeologists of ancient historical sites in Greece during 19th century. Another point to consider would be the architectural developments in Athens which, during the same period, began to use the classicist "language of forms" thus proclaiming a certain central-European image of antiquity. And in considering these exemplary two points one must also take into account that these "developments" were subject to local adaptations and revisions skewing the perception of a historical "authenticity". With reciprocal affinity, both western and local/diasporic classicism and romanticism shape the imaginary/aesthetic horizon which fashions the Greek attitude towards its history.

The exhibition and publication project *The Other designs*, adopts a critical viewpoint shared by many contemporary academics that highlight how the institutionalization of antiquity as "national heritage" has shaped an ideological framework for experiencing and performing a national identity. This viewpoint "kick-starts" an approach to the idea that nations such as Greece are in some way a multifaceted "assemblage", of constellated projections. *The Other designs*, aims to contribute to the current re-examination of historical authenticity by reflecting upon the status of national identity as a kind of "artistic" setup.

The publication contextualizing the exhibition consists of texts by Sofia Bempeza (Artist, Art Theorist and Assistant Professor for Art at Zurich University of Arts), Robin Klimecki (Lecturer, University of Bristol), Elpida Rikou (Anthropologist and Artist), Eleana Yalouri (Assistant Professor, Dept. of Social Anthropology, Panteion University of Social and Political Sciences) as well as of the curators of the exhibition Heiko Schmid (Assistant Professor for Art- and Cultural Theorie, Zurich University of Arts) and Kostis Stafylakis (Art Theorist, Teaching Fellow in "Research-based Art" at the Innovation and Entrepreneurship Unit of the Athens School of Fine Arts). The publication includes artistic inputs contributed by the artists Natasa Biza, Romy Rüegger, Zafos Xagoraris and Vassilis Vlastaras. The publication was developed by the artist Roland Regner as a contribution to the exhibition.

_Heiko Schmid & Kostis Stafylakis

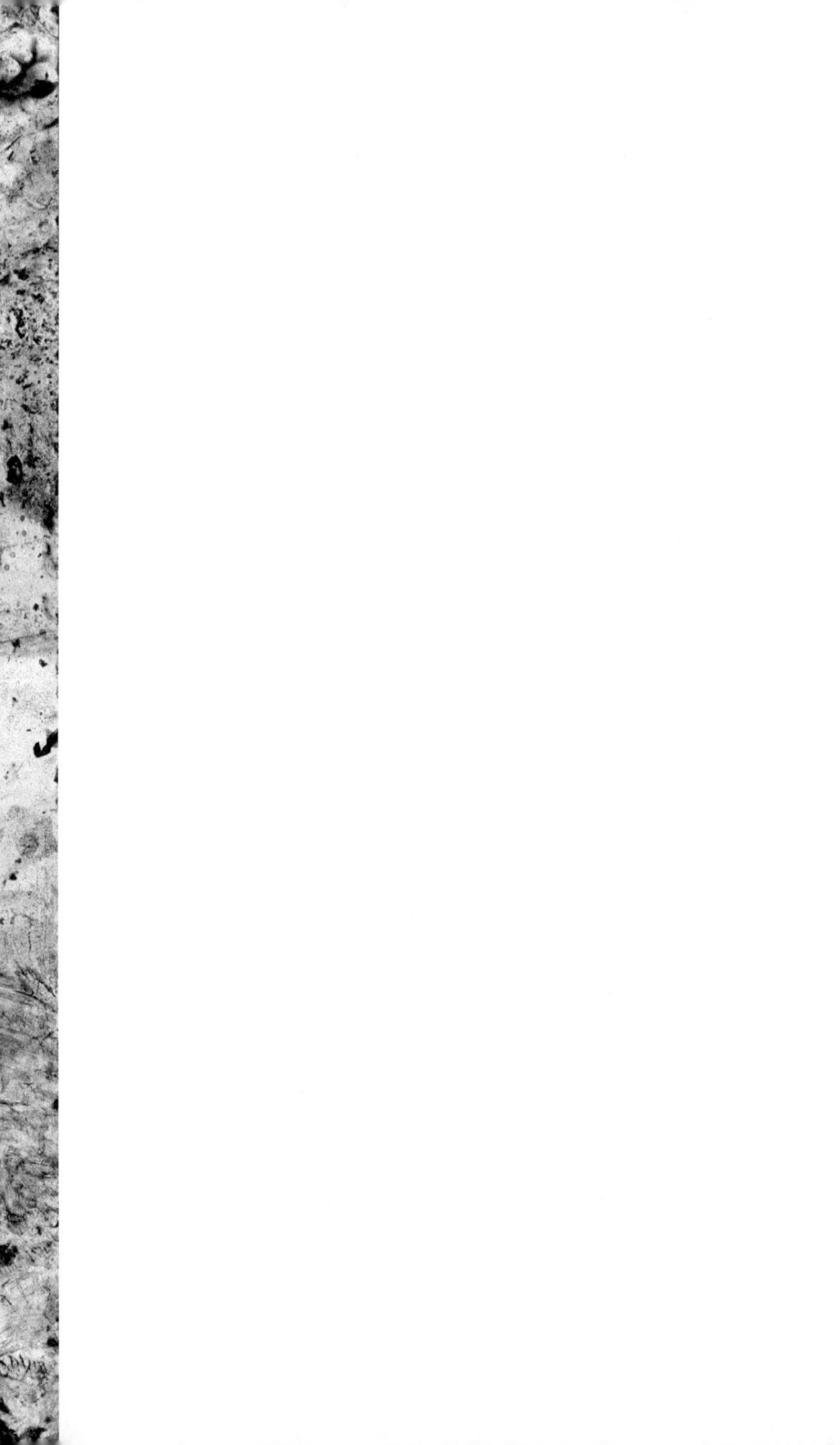

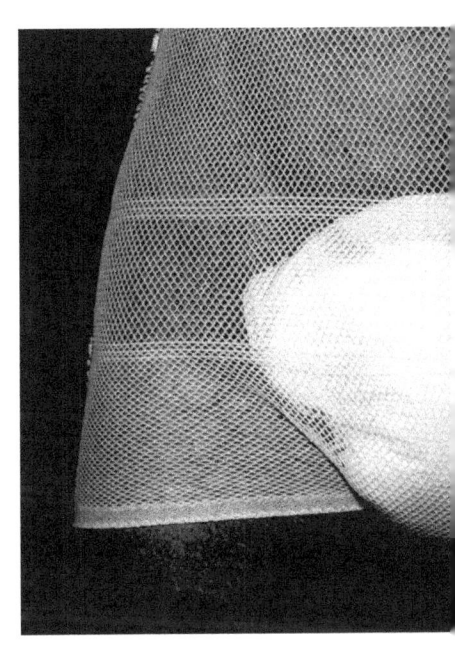

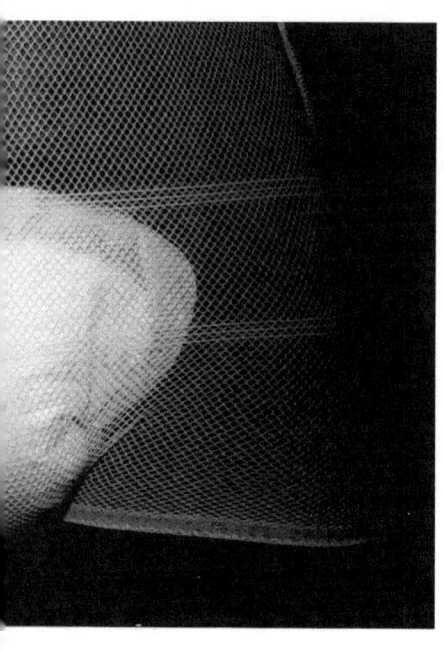

Notes on authenticity. The art of establishing historic narratives.

A few months before his death Walther Benjamin wrote his text *Über den Begriff der Geschichte* [Thesis on the Philosophy of History]. Benjamin in his *Thesis* emphasized his view of the past by questioning the widespread concept of a linear, time-line shaped history. For example in his V. Thesis Benjamin expresses the past as an "image", "which flashes up at the instant, when it can be recognized and is never seen again."[1] The past for Benjamin thus bases itself on ephemeral "imaginations". According to Benjamin's philosophy, we use unstable images to make the past become present and need signifiers to understand the opaque condition of time elapsing. And Benjamin in his *Thesis* even moves one step further by questioning whether history is concerned with something one could consider as past events? He states, that the way French protagonists viewed themselves as Rome reincarnates during the Revolution shows, that "history is the subject of a structure whose site is not homogeneous, empty time, but time filled by the presence of the now."[2] Benjamin comparable to contemporary philosophers like Cornelius Castoriadis, understands history as poiesis.[3] He defines history as a "field" of knowledge primarily construed by coevals. People such as Robespierre, according to Benjamin, primarily choose their historic references in order to explain and justify their actions.

With reference to this position, one must view history, especially if you are searching for authenticity, as a problematic "field" to deal with. In a Benjaminian perspective one would have to state that Robespierre knew the art of establishing historic narratives, due to him creating a set of "historic images" that helped to attain his goals. He was "choosing" his past in order to approximate a specific future. In the following text, with a Benjaminan perspective, I will look toward the evolutionary history of modern Greece highlighting how, in this country, imaginary interventions comparable to those of Robespierre took place.

To get this classification of contemporary Greek history across, it is paradoxically important to look beyond Greece and to name certain other developments, especially those which took place in 18th century central-Europe. The historian Walther Rehm in his

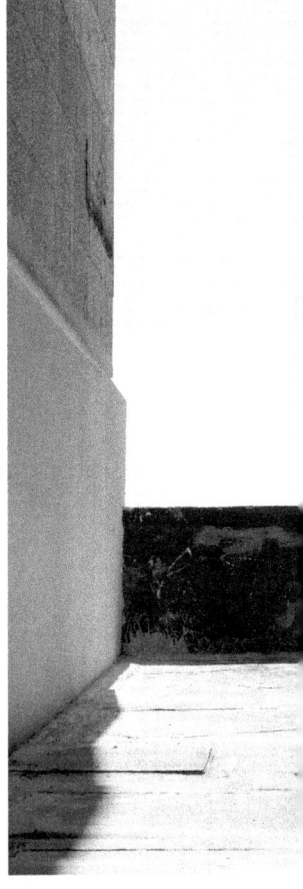

---

1   Walter Benjamin, Illuminations. New York 1968, p. 255.
2   Ibid., p. 261.
3   See Cornelius Castoriadis, Gesellschaft als imaginäre Institution. Entwurf einer politischen Philosophie. Frankfurt am Main 1984, p. 13.

famous book "Griechentum und Goethezeit"[4] for example points out, that the remains of the ancient Greek civilization, in historic Germany, were raised to the level of sacred manifestations.[5] In 18th century Germany, one can claim with Rehm, that a certain image of Greekness was established which was not specifically linked to Greece itself. There are several examples, proving that conceptions of Greek antiquity in the 18th century were used to develop the German idea of "Kulturnation" [cultural nation]. The proto art historian Johann Joachim Winckelmann, for instance, at this time started to publish his *Gedanken über die Nachahmung der griechischen Werke in der Malerey und Bildhauerkunst* [Thoughts on the Imitation of Greek Works in Painting and Sculpture], establishing classic Greek art

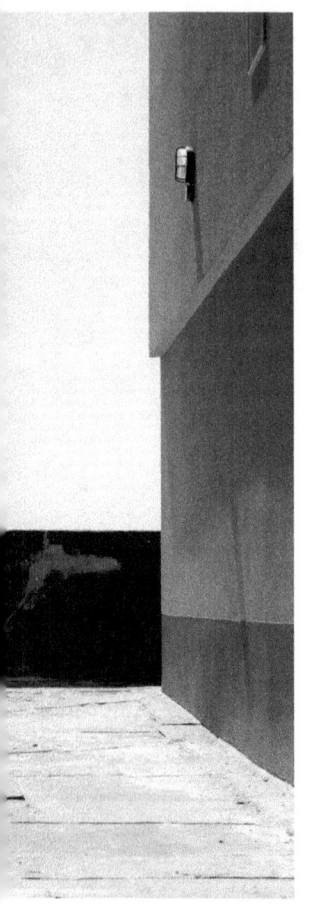

as a prototype for German art production. And 18th century was also the period when the Humboldtian "Bildungsreform" took place. Alexander von Humboldt during this period, as one can depict hereinafter, historically idealized the antique Hellenic culture to gain a kind of blueprint for a reform of the Prussian educational system. But what is the ideal meaning in this context? Humboldt himself in his text *Über das Studium des Alterthums* [On the academic studies of antiquity] claims that the original human „character" with the highest level of sophistication is manifested in that of the ancient Greek.[6] Studying Greek antiquity for Humboldt thus not only meant to determine the process of historical events but to use "imaginations" of a idealized Greek past to trace a way to the "source" of human culture itself. And this imperative classification of Greek antiquity also can be found in descriptions given by Walther Rehm. Rehm, for example, states that Friedrich Schiller's literary work was "ramming" through the layers of the Romanic mentality looking to expose the "archetype" of Greek thinking in confrontation to its (Roman and French) copies.[7] Aiming to unveil Greek history Rehm's argument, in a Humboldtian way, focuses on an approach toward cultural authenticity. It aims to get close to the source of human existence itself, to a quasi-religious alpha-point of (european) cultural identity. This exact line of reasoning is examined by the Greek/American historian Stathis Gourgouris, in his book *Dream Nation*. Gourgouris states that the classical "Bildung" for

---

4   It is not possible to translate this title. One possibly can describe this title as: the philosophic heritage of Greece in the times of Goethe.

5   Walther Rehm, Griechentum und Goethezeit. Geschichte eines Glaubens. Bern 1952, p 15.

6   See Wilhelm von Humboldt, Über das Studium des Altertums, und des Griechischen insbesondere, in: Schriften zu Altertumskunde und Ästhetik, edited by Andreas Flitner und Klaus Giel. Stuttgart 1961, p. 19.

7   See Walther Rehm, Griechentum und Goethezeit. Geschichte eines Glaubens. Bern 1952, p. 1.

Humboldt was not solely an appropriation of Greek culture but the Humboldtian "Bildung" also was: "its sublimation, which is to say, its reinscription with new social meaning, its resocialization."[8] Humboldt, as Gourgouris so is characterizing, was never aiming to give the Germans a Greek mentality. Greece for Humboldt, as well as his follower Rehm, represented some kind of ideal starting point. In his "Bildungsreform" Humboldt, via the image of antique Greek culture, tried to reshape Germany into a refuge for "authentic cultural existence".

The implication of "authentic cultural existence" within this context can be illustrated by the simple fact that neither Winkelmann nor Humboldt ever visited Greece themselves.

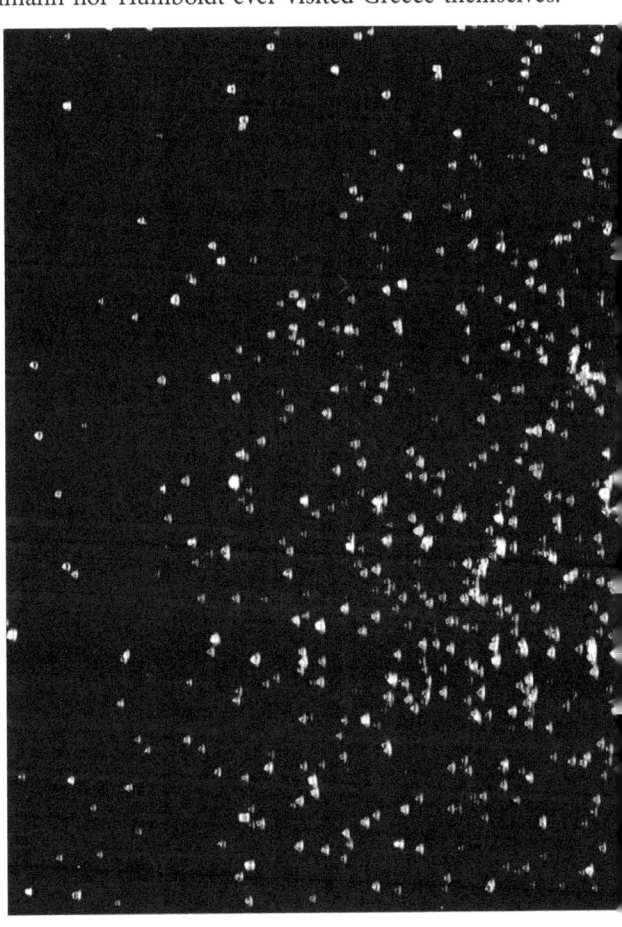

According to Rehm, the German "spirit" in the 18th century was developed separately from its Greek "body".[9] The question of how scholars like Winkelmann gained knowledge of classical Greek antiquity is explained by historian Suzanne L. Marchand. Marchand states that during the 18th century "handbooks on Greek history were not rare items in Europe"[10] and were broadly used by scholars. Neither Winkelmann nor Humboldt built a thesis based on their own observations but instead based on documentations they had attained. Though of course these handbooks must have had gaps of knowledge. Scholars like Winkelmann and Humboldt must had access to a lot of material, though the material only offered general outlines, but in its fragmentariness did provide "undetermined space" to build on their imaginations. One can claim from this perspective that

---

8   Stathis Gourghouris, Dream Nation. Enlightenment, Colonization, and the Institution of Modern Greece. Stanford 1996, p. 124.
9   See Walther Rehm, Griechentum und Goethezeit. Geschichte eines Glaubens. Bern 1952, p. 6.
10   Suzanne L. Marchand, Down from Olympus: archaeologie and philhellenism in Germany, 1750 – 1970. Princeton 1996, p. 6.

the historic idea of Greece developed by 18th century Germans was an image of longing construed in lonely studies. It represents to a greater extent the romantic conceptions of a number of ambitious scholars, then an entity, which may have been present during the course of history. Interestingly in the 18th century it was a writer who already seemed to be completely aware of this situation. According to Rehm, Johann Wolfgang Goethe in his Rome-letter claimed, that it is a misunderstanding that many of his coevals wished to be citizens of ancient cities like Athens. Goethe in his letter exemplified that the ideal of antiquity can only shine separate from the ignoble way one would definitely face while living in real Rome or Athens.[11] Historic approaches to understanding Greek antiquity in this sense,

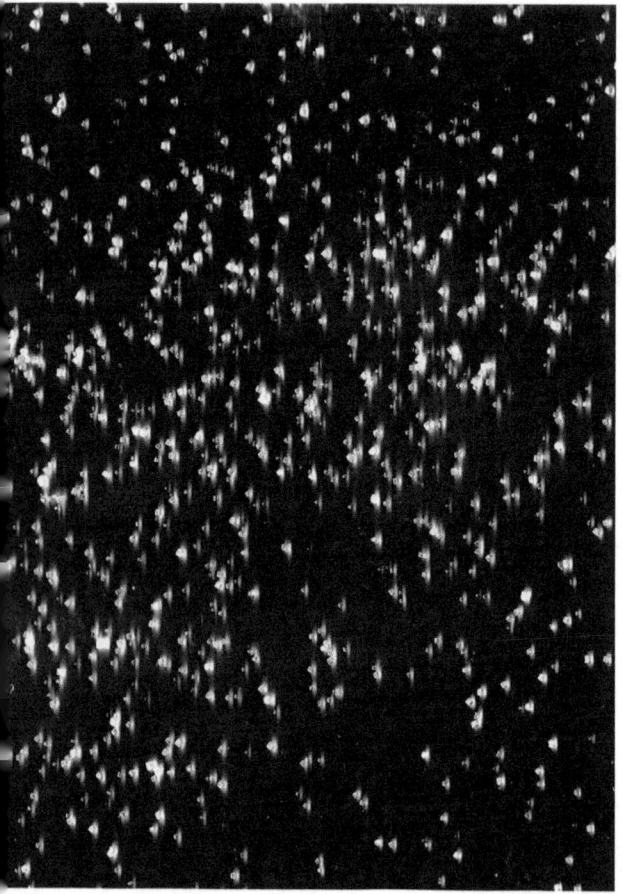

for decades took place without any contact to historic Greek regions of settlement. The "eternal Greek" as the historian Werner Oechslin states in his text *Unter dem griechischen Himmel...* [Under the sky of Greece...] is a purified central-European image, which was construed to render ideal living situations as possible.[12]

In reference to the implementation of a specific conception of Greek antiquity, a separation occurs between image and reality that has been noted by many (German) visitors to Greece (even in the 20th century), especially whilst visiting Greek monuments. A paradigmatic example in this context is an experience Sigmund Freud describes with relation to his 1904 trip to Athens. In a letter to his friend Romain Roland the psychologist illustrates a feeling of disbelief in the material reality of the Acropolis felt while stan-

---

11 See Walther Rehm, Griechentum und Goethezeit. Geschichte eines Glaubens. Bern 1952, p. 6.
12 See Werner Oechslin, „Unter dem griechischen Himmel...": Wirklichkeit und vor allem - Fiktion: Projektion und Strategien, in: Die griechische Klassik. Idee oder Wirklichkeit. edited by: Wolf-Dieter Heilmeyer. Berlin 2002, p. 685.

ding on top of the monument. "Concerning the evidence my senses are suggesting to me, I am on the Acropolis, but I can not believe it."[13] According to Freud the Acropolis, up until he was facing the monument, only represented a sheer possibility which furthermore should never be faced in reality.[14] What makes these descriptions relevant to this study is the fact that Freud is characterizing an irritation caused by an incongruity of an "image" within the actual presence of the landscape he walked in. Freud, in this description, one can suggest, shows himself as a typical "German Bildungsbürger". Freud understands that all he perceives is the truth, but is also intuitively aware of the situation that the Acropolis is also a "school-image", which has its own separate history and thereby its own reality. In other words: Freud uneasily experiences, how his purified central-European image of antiquity is getting contaminated or even overstruck by reality itself. He experiences a countryside, which is too concrete to remain in the status of a "Bildungs-ideal" that Freud was trained to believe in thereby causing him sincere feelings of alienation.

And this "disturbing presence" in Greece was still felt in the late 20th century. For example the German Philosopher Martin Heidegger in his book *Aufenthalte*[15] speaks of a "Traumschwelle" [dream barrier], which he feared to cross, during a planned visit to Greece.[16] According to Luise Michaelsen, the publisher of *Aufenthalte*, Heidegger even tried to avoid a visit to Greece being plagued by the doubt, "if in this country still an experience of the initial Greek" is possible.[17] He was thus questioning, if an approach toward an "authentic cultural presence" in Greece would at all be possible to achieve during a stay.

By taking into account both the positions of Freud and Heidegger, it is possible to depict the effects that historic projections, like those of Winkelmann and Humboldt (amongst others), can cause. These poetic classifications, that one can depict with reference to examples from Freud and Heidegger, changed themselves during the centuries to a status of documented knowledge,

---

14 Daß das Stück Realität, das wir ablehnen wollten, zunächst nur eine Möglichkeit war, bestimmte die Eigentümlichkeiten unserer damaligen Reaktion. Sigmund Freud, Brief an Romain Rolland, in: Gesammelte Werke. London 1950, p. 253.
15 In this book all notes Heidegger was producing during his stays in Greece are collected.
16 See Martin Heidegger, Aufenthalte. Frankfurt am Main 1989, p. 35.
17 Groß war die Scheu, die – stärker, als äußere Umstände es vermocht hätten – den Aufbruch immer wieder hinauszögerte. Und: Zunächst wollten die quälenden Zweifel, „ob je noch eine Erfahrung des anfänglich Griechischen gewährt sei", nicht verstummen. See Martin Heidegger, Aufenthalte. Frankfurt am Main 1989, p. 35.

to images that represent authenticity. These classifications manifested a certain "truth" that descendants of Winkelmann and Humboldt went searching for in a country whose classic scholars never visited. And the images they brought with them were for certain subject to local adaptions.

Up to our present day, one for example can describe the Greek appropriations of the classicist "language of forms" as having fashioned a collective attitude towards the cityscape in Athens, its architectural facade and its relation to the landscape. This is too extensive a topic to deliberate now and would require a separate text. But a striking example of these appropriations can be seen through nationalistic self-expressions of conservative Greeks concurrently common in both Greek and even German media. The nationalist Greeks, when expressing their opinions on the financial crisis, whether it be on TV-programs or newspapers, are repeatedly claiming that the Greek state should bowdlerize all the words and thoughts developed by its former "inhabitants". Confronted with a development like this, according to the interviewees, the Germans would revert back to a communicating with "animal cries". What makes these nationalistic positions relevant for this study is the situation that these statements have in being Greek appropriations of the established Humboldtian concept. According to the historian Christian Meier, there is no reason to assume that the ancient Greeks were considering their culture as fundamentally different from any other ancient high culture, for example the Egyptian.[18] Hence the previous statement cannot be traced back to Greek antiquity. In claiming that Greek history defines the "source" of human culture and knowledge itself, those interviewees so (unaware of the historicity of their viewpoint) are linking themselves to a central-European discourse on Greekness. I in this perspective would suggest that for many Greek nationalists a Humboldtian Idea represents a position relevant to their sense of self. These interviewees, in order to protect their cultural identity against "foreign invaders", are using an argumentative structure, which was created by 18th century Germans. In this way the Greek example offers the possibility to illustrate our concept of historic authenticity as a more multifaceted "assemblage", an outcome of constellated projections rather than a static time-line.

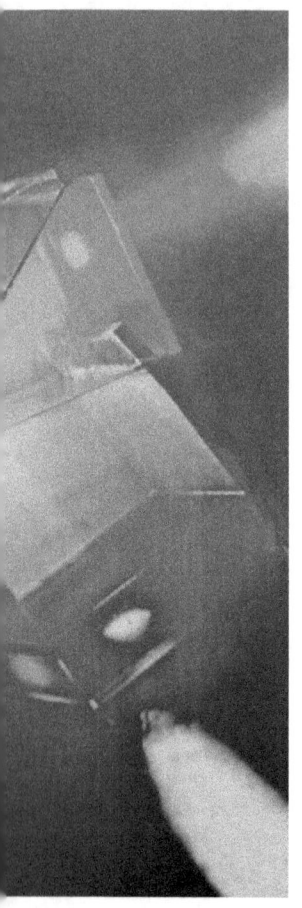

In discussing phenomena like the historic (re-)construction of

---

18 Christian Meier, A Culture of Freedom: Ancient Greece and the Origins of Europe. Oxford 2011, p. 37.

Greek antiquity, one can claim that Benjamin's description of the fabric of "history" must be even extended with further "structural layers", that aim to explain the interchange of imaginative determinations. History, as depicted in this text, is not only defined by the presence of actual interventions, but also by the determinates of past interpretations of historic situations especially concerning "the history of mentality" of societies. Historic imaginations so is highlighted, to a high level are defining our perceptions of authenticity and with this our identity. One so can show the art of establishing historic narratives by focusing on the historicity of idealized imaginations as a powerful, even mind setting occupation, that especially today awaits further systematic classification.

_Heiko Schmid

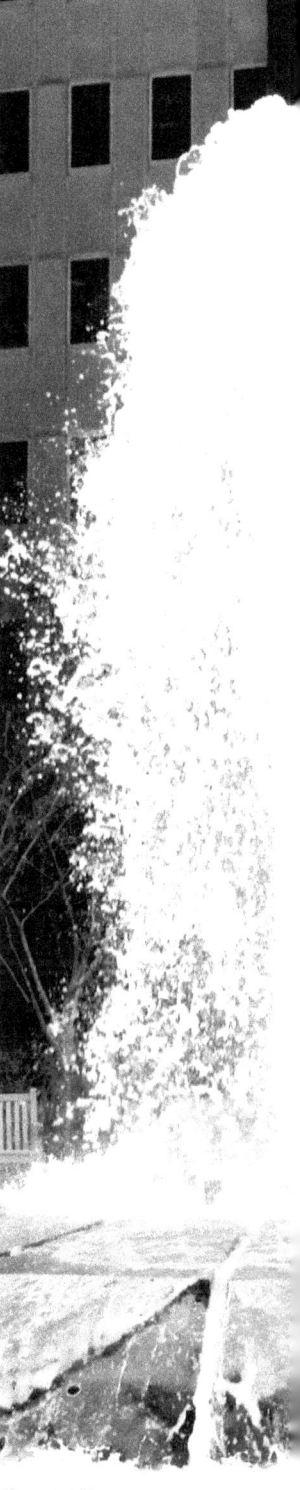

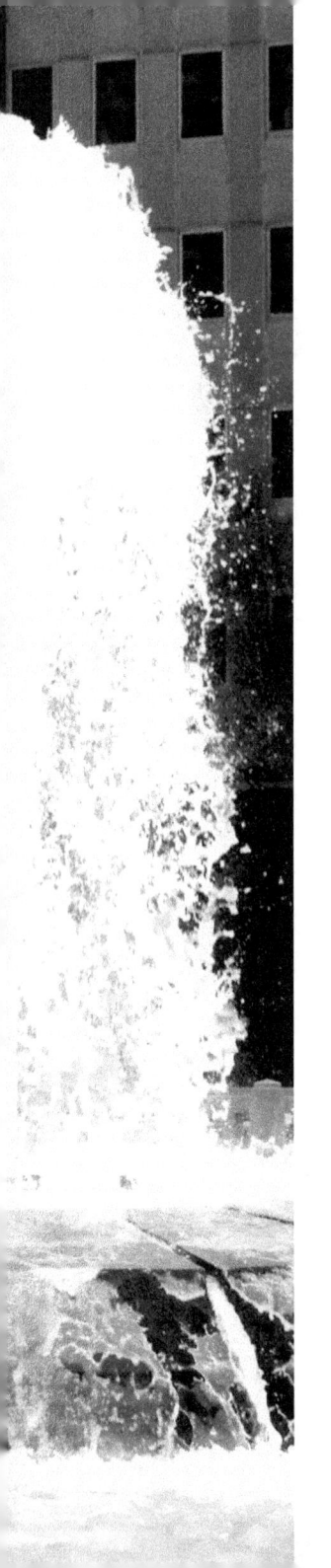

Reflections on the Greek Sovereign Debt Crisis and the Condition of the 'Indebted Man'

Introduction

This short essay investigates Maurizio Lazzarato's concept of the "indebted man"[1] in the context of the Greek sovereign debt crisis. In doing so, a particular focus is on how the rise of the "debt economy" has reconfigured subjectivity and power in the neoliberal era. The way that the crisis is discursively framed and acted upon can then be seen as an attempt to expand and intensify the condition of the indebted man rather than as an opportunity to reassess our priorities. While the Greek crisis has often been presented as an exemplary case, my aim is to use it as an example in order to illuminate some of the characteristics of the contemporary neoliberal conjuncture that we all find ourselves in.

Debt and Subjectivity

As Lazzarato[2] has pointed out, debt has been a defining logic of neoliberalism since its emergence. The recent financial crises (by which he roughly refers to the period between the dotcom crash and the European sovereign debt crisis) have now fully revealed the contours of this "debt economy" within which the subjective figure of the "indebted man"[3] though always having been present, has now superseded (or perhaps better: subsumed) Foucault's "entrepreneur of the self" as the defining figure of the neoliberalist era. The condition of the indebted man is one where neoliberalism's grand subjective promises of: "everyone a shareholder, everyone an owner, everyone an entrepreneur"[4], have increasingly turned into the (equally subjective) command to manage the costs and risks of financial, economic and political failure and collapse. Therefore contemporary "work on the self" under neoliberalism first and foremost means to take charge of the debt (in its various forms and guises) that ca-

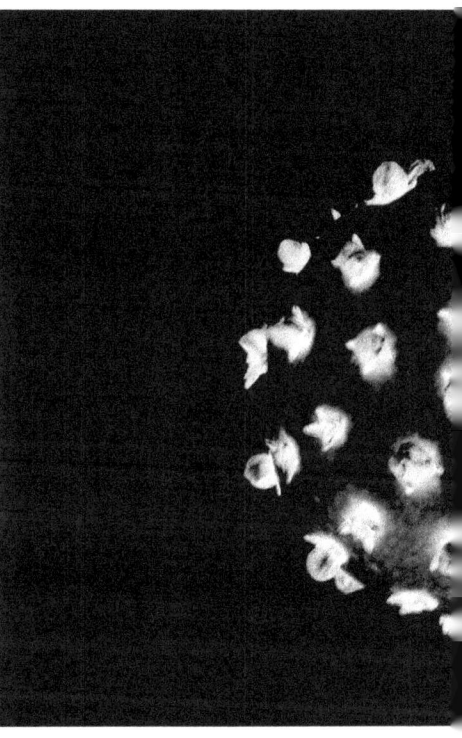

---

[1] Maurizio Lazzarato, The Making of the Indebted Man. Cambridge, Mass: Semiotext(e)/MIT Press. 2012.
[2] Ibid.
[3] This gendered notion of the 'indebted man' is of course not ideal but I will use it throughout this essay for the sake of consistency.
[4] Maurizio Lazzarato, The Making of the Indebted Man. Cambridge, Mass: Semiotext(e)/MIT Press. 2012 p. 9.

pitalism has externalised onto society. Debt and credit are hereby not mere economic categories based on equal exchange but relations of power that cut across all other relations of exploitation and domination to the point that now everyone is a "debtor", accountable to a guilty before capital.[5]

The debt economy is subjective in the sense that it functions to produce individual and collective subjectivities at the level of the economic infrastructure[6] and also moral since moral categories such as guilt, duty, blame, conscience etc. are inscribed into a creditor-debtor relationship from the beginning. As Friedrich Nietzsche points out, the German word for debt is guilt (Schuld)[7] after all. Indeed for Nietzsche, the relation between creditors and debtors is the archetype of social relations wherein person met person for the first time and measured himself person against person.[8]

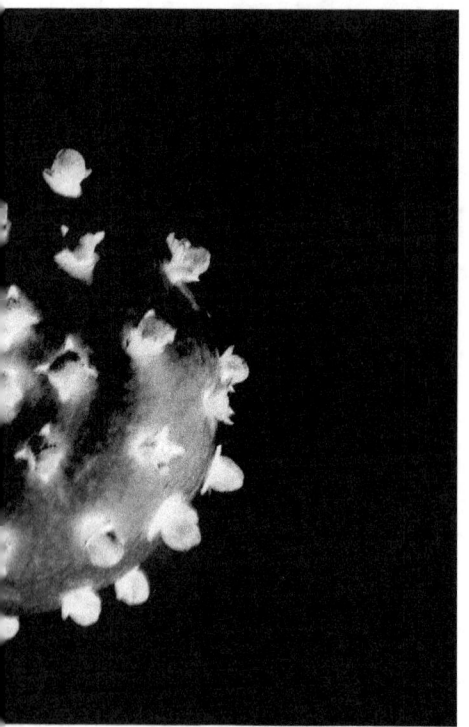

The indebted man, then, becomes both individually (or as a group or population) responsible for honouring his debts as well as being morally at fault for having entered the debt relationship in the first place. However, the moral injunction that "one has to honour one's debts" does not apply to everyone in equal measure and historically never has.[10] Not everyone has to repay his or her debts! It is therefore useful to investigate how certain discourses capitalise on, and amplify, this "violence of guilt engendered by debt"[11] in regards to targeting particular subjects and not others. The German newspaper campaign against Greece led by the German tabloid newspaper Bild Zeitung is illustrative in this regard as it blends the notion of the morality of

	5	Maurizio Lazzarato, The Making of the Indebted Man. Cambridge, Mass: Semiotext(e)/ MIT Press. 2012 p. 7.
	6	Maurizio Lazzarato, Signs and Machines: Capitalism and the Production of Subjectivity. Cambridge, Mass: Semiotext(e)/ MIT Press 2014.
7		In fact, this is the case for a large number historical languages. See David Graeber, Debt: The First 5.000 Years. Brooklyn, NY: Melville House 2011.
8		Cited in Maurizio Lazzarato, The Making of the Indebted Man. Cambridge, Mass: Semiotext(e)/MIT Press 2012, p.39; original emphasis.
9		It is perhaps useful to limit this notion to the specific morality of bourgeois society only as proposed by Graeber (2011, chapter 5) since there have always been other, often more communitarian, ways of conceptualising community, morality and economic relationships.
10		David Graeber, Debt: The First 5.000 Years. Brooklyn, NY: Melville House 2011
11		Maurizio Lazzarato, The Making of the Indebted Man. Cambridge, Mass: Semiotext(e)/ MIT Press 2012.

debt and the legitimacy of punishment with racial and national stereotypes which has created a forceful narrative frame that, in turn, has underpinned more official discourses and responses to the Greek crisis.[12]

During 2010 and 2011 particularly, Bild published countless articles and features under the heading of "bankrupt Greeks" ("Pleite-Griechen")[13] to force Greece "to repay all of their debts" and/or leave the Eurozone. This campaign culminated in the transgressive demand to "sell your islands, you bankrupt greeks … and the Acropolis as well!"[14]

In juxtaposing the figure of the corrupt, lazy and tax-evading (yet better paid) Greek with that of the hard-working, thrifty and diligent German who will have to pick up the tab for the former's excesses, the campaign constructed a crisis narrative that individualised blame and guilt and held the Greek population responsible for all of their domestic problems as well as for the European crisis more generally while at the same time downplaying broader systemic and structural causes of the meltdown.[15]

"Bankrupt Greeks" served as a master signifier for a range of racially inflected discourses that organised desire and affect by positing the Greek population as the "Other" who "steals our enjoyment" to put it in Lacanian terms. "Ultimately, what bothers you in the Other" as Slavoj Žižek[16] puts it, is the way that he or she enjoys. Moreover, "bankrupt Greeks" are not just "enjoying" themselves, they do so at the expenses of the German taxpayer.[17] Here, the typecasting of Greeks as the quintessential scapegoats who are responsible for the theft of enjoyment follows

---

12 See Yiannis Mylonas, Media and the Economic Crisis of the EU: The "Culturalization" of a Systemic Crisis and Bild-Zeitung's Framing of Greece. Communication, Capitalism & Critique 10 (2) 2012, pp. 646-671.

13 *The Bild Zeitung* has been at the forefront of this campaign. However, the coverage of other German newspapers particuraly *Focus* and *Der Spiegel* has been similarly negative (Schlosser), 2013.

14 *Bild Zeitung* Sell Your Islands You Bankrupt Greeks, 27 October 2010, available at: http://www.bild.de/politik/wirtschaft/griechenland-krise/regierung-athen-sparen-verkauft-inseln-pleite-akropolis-11692338.bild.html, accessed 24 August, 2014.

15 Yiannis Mylonas, Media and the Economic Crisis of the EU: The "Culturalization" of a Systemic Crisis and Bild-Zeitung's Framing of Greece. Communication, Capitalism & Critique 10 (2) 2012, pp. 646-671.

16 Slavoj Žižek, It Doesn't Have to Be a Jew – Slavoj Žižek Interviewed by Josefina Ayerza, Lusitania 1 (4) 1994, available at: http://www.lacan.com/perfume/Zizekinter.htm, accessed 20 August, 2014.

17 What is conveniently 'forgotten' in this type of narrative is that taxpayers will only be called upon in the case of default and have so far not paid anything towards the bailout of Greece or another European country.

established tropes and patterns in the popular press that are aimed at mobilising affect and desire in order to attain closure which can lend themselves to particular political projects.[18] From this point of view, the stigmatization and shaming of "bankrupt Greeks" can be seen as partaking in a "restorative fantasmatic narrative" which aims at recuperating the neoliberalist status quo and marginalising contestation and alternatives by deflecting attention away from wider systemic issues through scapegoating and the individualisation of blame.[19] This type of narrativisation has served the German government, and Angela Merkel in particular, rather well as it has allowed for the portrayal of a determined and steely type of leadership by pushing for harsh austerity measures as a condition of the bailout. It is thus that the "imaginary promise of recapturing our lost/impossible enjoyment"[20] in the German press (i.e. the imagined return to prosperity and well-being upon removal of the "Greek threat" to German stability, wealth and pride) has provided the affective support for neo-imperialist strategies that are principally aimed at furthering the condition of the indebted man as a we shall see below.

Debt as a Machine of Extraction and Domination
According to Lazzarato,[21] the debt economy reconfigures power relationships and modes of economic governance as well as capital accumulation in a fundamental way. In addition to the production and "government" of individual and collective subjectivities, it acts as a "capture", "predation" and "extraction" machine on the whole of society, as an instrument for macroeconomic prescription and management, and as a mechanism for income redistribution".

The austerity measures administered by many governments in the wake of the crisis and in particular in the European periphery as a condition of their bailouts - Greece most of all - serves as an opportunity for neoliberalist restructuring and the subjection of whole populations to a form of "debt peonage". Arguably, these developments

---

18 Wei-yuan Chang and Jason Glynos, Ideology and Politics in the Popular Press, in: Dahlberg, L. and Phelan, S. (eds.): Discourse Theory and Critical Media Politics. Basingstoke: Palgrave MacMillan, 2011, pp. 106-127.
19 Cf Jason Glynos, Robin Klimecki and Hugh Willmott, Cooling Out the Marks: The Identity and Politics of the Financial Crisis. Journal of Cultural Economy 5 (3) 2012, pp. 297-320.
20 Yannis Stavrakakis, Passions of Identification, in: Howarth, David and Torfing, Jacob (eds): Discourse Theory in European Politics: Identity, Policy and Governance. Basingstoke: Palgrave MacMillan 2005, p. 73.
21 Maurizio Lazzarato, The Making of the Indebted Man. Cambridge, Mass: Semiotext(e)/MIT Press 2012, p.29.

on of neoliberalism[22] that resembles feudalist relations of power in the sense that "a portion of labor is owed in advance, as serf labour, to the feudal lord".[23]
Against this background, neoliberalism aims to continuously perpetuate and intensify the condition of the indebted man. Here, debt emerges not (or not predominantly) as a problem but as a "solution of sorts",[24] i.e. a mechanism of domination and governance. We are arguably currently facing a "state of permanent economic emergency"[25] within which the "state of exception",[26] i.e. the crisis of debt itself, has been elevated into the primary governing principle. This is particularly apparent in Greece, as, according to the Memorandum signed by the Greek government, the European Union and the IMF, they are essentially obliged to do whatever is necessary to attain fiscal balance. As a result, "open field has effectively been declared on Greek economy and society" as Costas Lapavistas et al.[27] put it.

The humanitarian catastrophe that has unfolded in Greece as a result of austerity bears witness to the fact that this has had significant biopolitical implications. What is increasingly at stake, it seems, is "bare life", i.e. a decision on the value or non-value of life itself[28] in which certain subjects can be stripped of any protection and dignity.[29] In Greece this appears to be particularly the case for migrants who, even more so than ordinary citizens, suffer from the effects of

---

22	Ian Bruff, The Rise of Authoritarian Neoliberalism. *Rethinking Marxism: A Journal of Economics, Culture and Society* 26 (1) 2013, pp. 113-129.
23	Jean Baudrillard cited in Maurizio Lazzarato, The Making of the Indebted Man. Cambridge, Mass: Semiotext(e)/MIT Press 2012, p. 13.
24	Yannis Stavrakakis, Debt Society: Greece and the Future of Post-Democracy. *Radical Philosophy* 181 (Sept/Oct) 2013, pp. 34.
25	Slavoj Žižek, A Permanent Economic Emergency. *New Left Review* 64 (July/Aug) 2010, pp. 85-95.
26	Giorgio Agamben, Homo Sacer: Sovereign Power and Bare Life. Stanford: Stanford University Press 1998. Giorgio Agamben, State of Exception. Chicago: Chicago University Press 2005.
27	Costas Lapavitsas et al, Crisis in the Eurozone. London: Verso 2012, p.120.
28	Giorgio Agamben, Homo Sacer: Sovereign Power and Bare Life. Stanford: Stanford University Press 1998.
29	See also Simon Orpana and Evan Mauro, First as Tragedy, then as Ford: Performing the Biopolitical Image in the Age of Austerity, from the G20 to Toronto City Hall. Topia 30-31 2013/14, pp. 271-289.

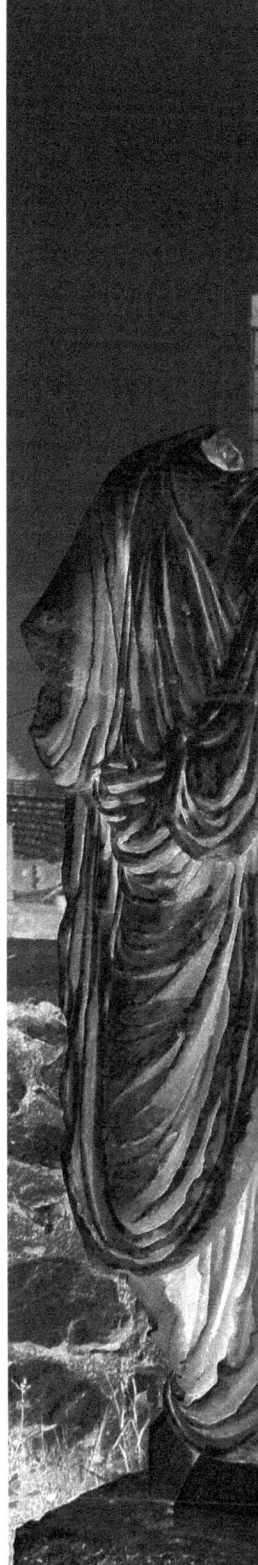

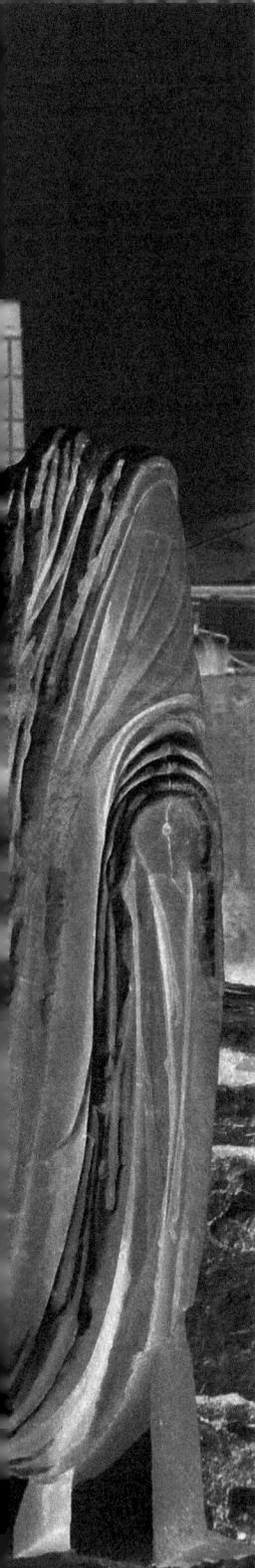

austerity and are also increasingly victims of racist attacks which, as a publication by PICUM[30] emphasises, challenges "their most fundamental right: their right to life".

As indicated above, the debt economy also reconfigures the ways that capitalism extracts value from the economy. In doing so, profits are increasingly accumulated through processes of financialization, i.e. the investment of profits through financial channels.[31] Again, the crisis and its accompanying austerity initiatives offer a way of furthering and intensifying this agenda via neoliberal restructuring.

One of the central mechanisms through which this occurs is captured by the term "accumulation by dispossession".[32] This refers to the neo-imperialist (as well as domestic) strategies of many Western countries, in the neoliberalist era, to open up new sectors for capital accumulation by dispossessing the public of its wealth, land and ownership of the means of production, e.g. through privatisation, financialization/deregulation and other redistributive policies which typically involve a transfer of wealth from the many to the few.

Debt plays a crucial role in this, as international debt crises over the past decades have traditionally been used to enforce neoliberal restructuring of the economies of debtor states by international bodies such as the IMF and the World Bank.[33] The drastic austerity measures imposed on Greece and enforced by the "troika" such as severe spending and wage cuts, tax raises and substantial privatisation and deregulation initiatives (which have been heavily directed against labour) are therefore consistent with neoliberalism's tendency towards "debt imperialism" as well as a more general tendency of capitalism

---

30 PICUM, The Silent Humanitarian Crisis in Greece: Devising Strategies to Improve the Situation of Migrants in Greece, Work shop Report, p. 6, available at: http://picum.org/picum.org/uploads/publication/The%20Silent%20Humanitarian%20Crisis%20in%20Greece%20Devising%20Strategies%20to%20Improve%20the%20Situation%20of%20Migrants%20in%20Greece%202012.pdf, accessed 25 September, 2014.

31 Greta Krippner, The Financialization of the American Economy. Socio-Economic Review 3(2) 2005, pp. 178-208. Giovanni Arrighi, The Long Twentieth Century: Money, Power and the Origins of Our Time. 2nd Ed. London: Verso 2009.

32 David Harvey, The New Imperialism. Oxford: OUP 2003.

33 See also Tayyab Mahmud, Is It Greek Or Déjà vu All Over Again?: Neoliberalism and Winners and Losers of International Debt Crises. Loyola University Chicago Law Journal 42 (4) 2011, pp. 629-712.

to prey on disaster, shocks and human catastrophe.[34]
Historically, there is scant evidence that austerity has ever delivered on its promises[35] and it has certainly failed in Greece.[36] I therefore argue that the way the European sovereign debt crisis has thus far been resolved (at the interrelated levels of discourse, economic structure and politics) is first and foremost a form of "government" and control directed at a recuperation of the neoliberalist project and an intensification of the "condition of the indebted man" which involves the targeting of particular groups and populations as scapegoats. The figure of the "bankrupt Greek" therefore serves a particular ideological and political strategy in order to obfuscate contingency and legitimate exploitation.

Public protest and counter-discourses have not (yet) been translated into a credible challenge of the neoliberalist status quo. Indeed, some commentators have pointed to the rise of a "post-democratic" or even potentially "anti-democratic" society engendered by the violence and "universal cruelty" inherent in the debt economy.[37] If there is a silver lining, it is perhaps that we all share the condition of the indebted man; In fact, it is debt that binds us all together.[38] It is therefore worth emphasising with David Graeber[39] that "debt is just the perversion of a promise". If we were collectively to start questioning the "sacred principle" that debts need to be repaid, we might, at some point, be able to commit the indebted man, including its particular incarnation of the "bankrupt Greek", to the flames.

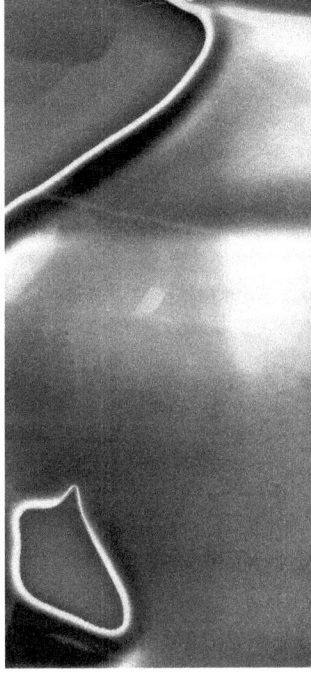

_Robin Klimecki

---

34 Naomi Klein, The Shock Doctrine. London: Penguin, Allen Lane 2007.
35 Mark Blyth, Austerity: The History of a Dangerous Idea. Oxford: OUP 2013.
36 Costas Lapavitsas et al, Crisis in the Eurozone. London: Verso 2012.
37 See the discussion in Yannis Stavrakakis, Debt Society: Greece and the Future of Post-Democracy. Radical Philosophy 181 (Sept/Oct) 2013, pp. 33-38.
38 See Richard Dienst, The Bonds of Debt: Borrowing Against the Common Good. London: Verso 2011.
39 David Graeber, Debt: The First 5.000 Years. Brooklyn, NY: Melville House 2011, p.391.

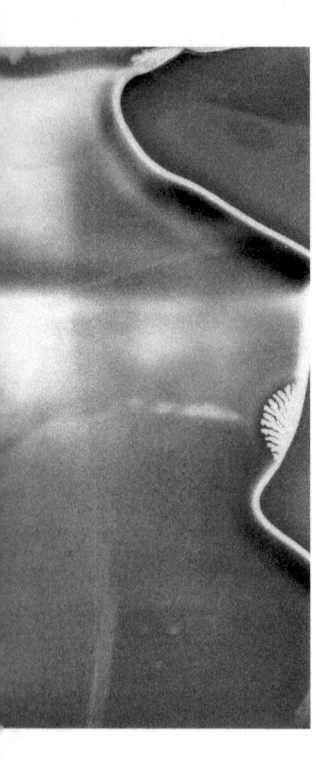

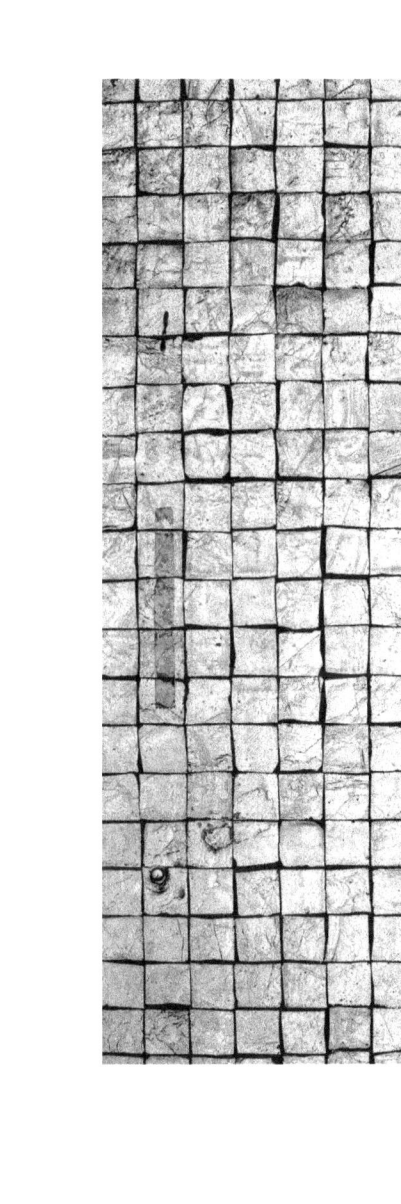

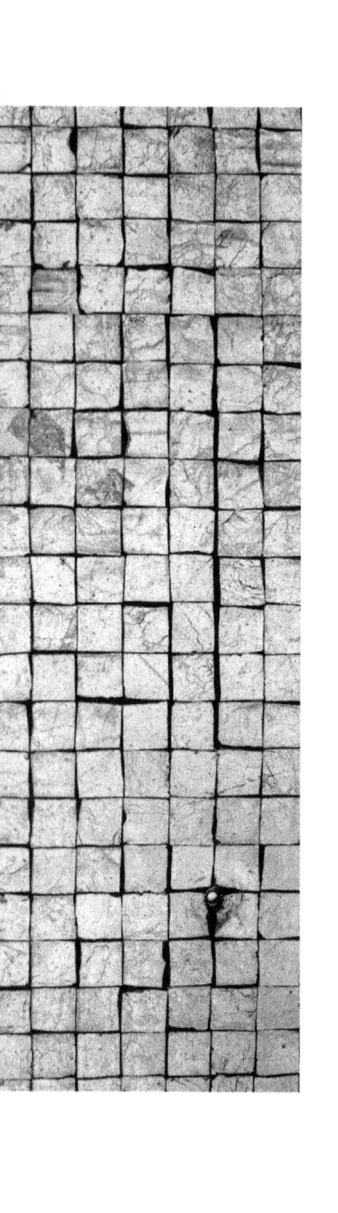

ΣΧΕΔΙΟΝ ΠΕΡΙ ΑΝΑΒΑΘΜΙΣΕΩΣ ΤΟΥ ΚΕΝΤΡΟΥ ΤΗΣ ΠΟΛΕΩΣ ΤΩΝ ΑΘΗΝΩΝ ΚΑΘΩΣ ΚΑΙ ΤΗΣ ΑΝΑΚΑΙΝΗΣΕΩΣ ΤΟΥ ΒΑΣΙΛΙΚΟΥ ΟΙΚΟΥ ΤΗΣ ΑΚΡΟΠΟΛΕΩΣ

ΥΠΟ ΤΟΥ ΚΑΘΗΓΗΤΟΥ
ΑΠΟΣΤΟΛΟΥ ΔΕΚΑΒΑΛΑ
ΓΕΝΙΚΟΥ ΓΡΑΜΜΑΤΕΩΣ
ΤΟΥ ΥΠΟΥΡΓΕΙΟΥ ΑΝΑΠΤΥΞΕΩΣ

ΕΙΣ ΜΝΗΜΗΝ ΤΟΥ ΗΡΩΟΣ
ΚΑΙ ΕΝΔΟΞΟΥ ΣΤΡΑΤΗΓΟΥ
ΕΙΣ ΤΑ ΠΕΔΙΑ ΤΩΝ ΜΑΧΩΝ
ΔΕΚΑΒΑΛΑ ΛΑΜΠΡΟΥ

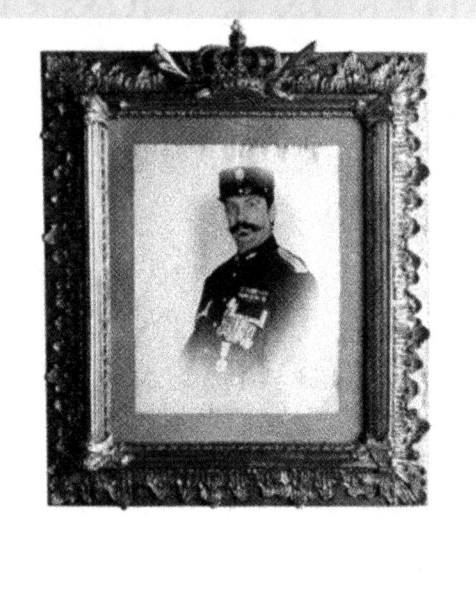

ΕΠΙΜΕΛΕΙΑ: καθ. ΑΠΟΣΤΟΛΟΣ ΔΕΚΑΒΑΛΑΣ
ΕΠΙΜΕΤΡΟΝ: ΠΕΡΙΚΛΗΣ ΓΙΑΝΝΟΠΟΥΛΟΣ
ΜΕΛΕΤΗ ΕΡΓΟΥ: KARL FRIEDRICH
SCHINKEL PROJECT OFFICE LTD.

Ἡμεῖς οἱ Ἕλληνες, ἀγνοοῦμεν τὴν Ἑλλάδα καὶ τὸν Ἕλληνα, περισσότερον κάθε Κίνας κάθε Κινέζου. Φανταζόμεθα τὸν ἑαυτόν μας κα ὶ τὸν τόπον μας, ἀπὸ τὰ γράμματα ποὺ μᾶς στέλλουν οἱ Εὐρωπαῖοι, οἱ ὁ ποῖοι μᾶς ἀγνοοῦν ἐντελέστατα. Καὶ εἰς τὴν ἰδικήν μας ὑπνοβατικὴν κατάστασιν καὶ εἰς τὴν ἰδικὴν μας παραφροσύνην, προστίθενται καὶ αἱ ε ὐρωπαϊκαὶ ἐξωφρενικαὶ γνῶμαι καὶ συμβουλαὶ καὶ μᾶς ἀποτρελλαίνουν τελειωτικῶς, χαπτόμεναι ὅπως χάπτεται ἡ κάθε γνώμη τοῦ κάθε Δίτεριχ ἢ Μίντεριχ, τοῦ ὁποίου τοῦ καπνίζει νὰ μᾶς φωτίσῃ καὶ μᾶς συμβουλεύσῃ καὶ μᾶς βάλῃ νόμον εἰς τὸ σπίτι μας καὶ μᾶς ὁδηγήσῃ εἰς τὸν δρόμον μας, σὰν νὰ εἴμεθα ἐμεῖς στραβοὶ καὶ παραλυτικοί. Ὅλαι μας λοιπὸν αἱ ἰδέαι, ὁ χωρισμὸς τῶν Ἰδανικῶν εἰς Ἀρχαϊσμὸν καὶ Κλεφτισμόν, ὅλη ἡ παραφροσύνη τοῦ γλωσσικοῦ ζητήματος, ἡ κάθε ἄγνοια καὶ ἡ κάθε ξενομανία, ἡ τελεία σύγχισις καὶ ἀνεμοζάλη κάθε ἰδέας καὶ κάθε πράγματος, ἐκεῖ ἔχει τὴν ἀληθῆ πηγήν της.

Πᾶσα σκέψις, γνώμη, ζήτησις ἰδικοῦ μας ἢ ξένου σοφοῦ, εἴτε περὶ τῶν Μυθολογικῶν χρόνων μας εἴτε περὶ τῶν τωρινῶν, ἀπὸ τὴν μίαν ἄκραν τῆς Ἑλληνικῆς Ἱστορίας μέχρι τῆς ἄλλης εἰς οἱονδήποτε ζήτημα, εἴτε παρελθόν, εἴτε τωρινὸν δύναται νὰ εἶναι περίφημον ὡς ὑλικὸν ἀλλὰ δὲν ἔχει καμμίαν ἀξίαν καὶ δὲν πρέπει νὰ κάμνῃ καμμίαν ἐντύπωσιν, διότι ὅ λα του τὰ συμπεράσματα δὲν ἔχουν καμμίαν θετικὴν βάσιν, εἶναι μόνον χρονογραφικὴ ἐργασία, ἐνόσῳ δὲν παρουσιάζουν τὴν γνῶσιν τοῦ τωρινοῦ Ἕλληνος καὶ ὁ τωρινὸς Ἕλλην εἶναι ἄγνωστος εἰς τοὺς ξένους.

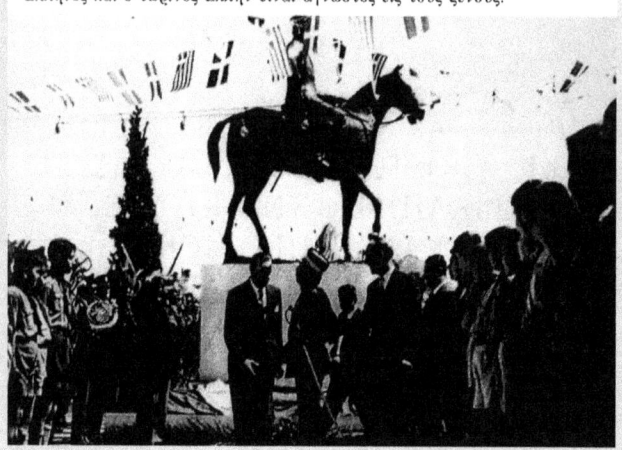

Καὶ ὅσον ἀφορᾷ τοὺς Εὐρωπαίους τοὺς οἱουσδήποτε, ἔστω καὶ ἀ καδημαϊκούς, ἕνας Ἕλλην ἔχει τὸ θάρρος νὰ τοὺς εἰπῇ, ὅτι εἶναι ἀπρεπὲς καὶ ἀδικαιολόγητον, ἐνῷ τοιοῦτον βαθὺ ἐπιστημονικὸν πνεῦμα βασιλεύει εἰς τὴν Εὐρώπην, εἰς κάθε ζήτησιν, νὰ ἐφαρμόζονται εἰς τὴν ἑλληνικὴν ζήτησιν, κατ᾽ ἐξαίρεσιν μοναδικήν, τόσον παιδαριωδῶς ἐπιπόλαια συστήματα, καὶ νὰ ἐπιδεικνύεται τοιαύτη τόλμη πεποιθήσεως καὶ συμπερασμάτων, ἐπὶ πραγμάτων τόσον μακρυνῶν καὶ ἀγνώστων.

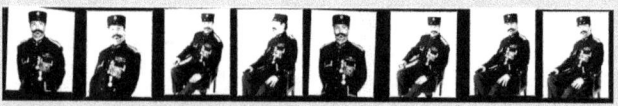

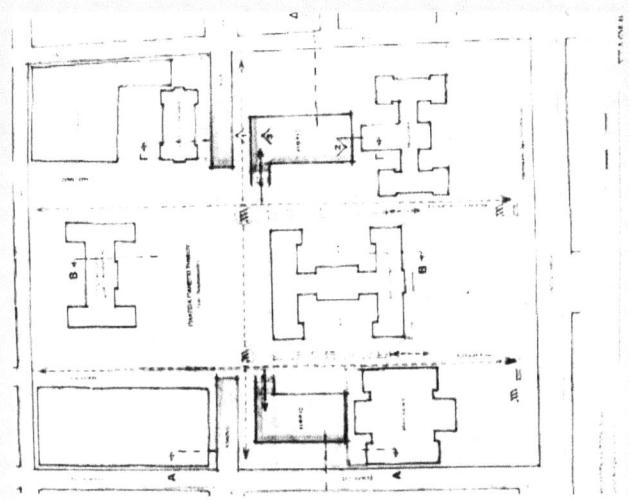

Ὑπάρχει ἕνα καθῆκον εἰς τὸν τόπον αὐτόν. Καὶ τὸ καθῆκον αὐτὸ εἶναι νὰ μελετήσωμεν ἡμεῖς αὐτοὶ τὸν ἑαυτόν μας, τὸ παρελθόν μας, τὸ παρόν μας, δι ἁ νὰ γνωρίζωμεν τί εἴμεθα καὶ τί δυνάμεθα νὰ κάμωμεν καὶ πρὸς ποίας ὁδοὺς νὰ βαδίσωμεν καὶ πρὸς τί αὔριον, πρὸς ποῖον προσεχὲς καὶ ποῖον ἀπώτερον μέλλον, νὰ μελετήσωμεν καὶ ἀναλύσωμεν τὴν γύρω ἡμῶν πραγματικὴν ζωήν, τοὺς ἀνθρώπους καὶ τὰ ἔργα των διὰ νὰ γνωρίζωμεν τί σημαίνουν αὐτὰ καὶ τ ί λέγομεν ἡμεῖς. Τὸ καθῆκον αὐτὸ ἐπέβαλα πρῶτον εἰς ἐμαυτόν. Καὶ κατὰ τὴν φύσιν καὶ παρὰ τὴν κλίσιν καὶ ἐναντίον τῆς ψυχικῆς διαθέσεως ἐδέσμευσα τὰ ς καλλιτεχνικάς μου δυνάμεις καὶ ὁρμὰς πρὸς ἐκδήλωσιν, διὰ νὰ ἐκτελέσω πρ ῶτον αὐτό.

Τὸ Ἑλληνικὸν Πνεῦμα τοῦ λήγοντος ἀπὸ τοῦ Ἀγῶνος Αἰῶνος -Πνεῦμα Ἀ ερολογικὸν- ἐφάνη Ἀνικανώτατον νὰ ἐννοήσῃ τὴν: ΕΛΛΗΝΙΚΗΝ ΑΝΘΡΩΠΟΤΗΤΑ. Τὸ Ἑλληνικὸν Πνεῦμα τοῦ λήγοντος Αἰῶνος, ἐφάνη Ἀ νικανώτατον νὰ ἐννοήσῃ σαφῶς, πρῶτον τὴν Φυσιολογίαν τοῦ Ἕλληνος καὶ δεύτερον τὴν Φυσιολογίαν τῆς Ἑλληνικῆς Φυλῆς, ἵνα διὰ τῶν δύο μοναδικῶν αὐτῶν ριζικῶν μέσων, ἐννοήσῃ τὸ Παρελθὸν Αὐτῆς ὁλόκληρον μέχρι τῆς Ἐ παναστάσεως, καθὼς καὶ τὸ Παρόν, οὕτω δὲ ἐκ τῆς τριπλῆς γνώσεως, ἀσφαλῶ ς ὁδηγούμενον, διαγράψῃ Σαφέστατα, τὰς Βάσεις τῆς Δημιουργίας τοῦ: ΝΕΟΥ ΕΛΛΗΝΙΚΟΥ ΚΟΣΜΟΥ.

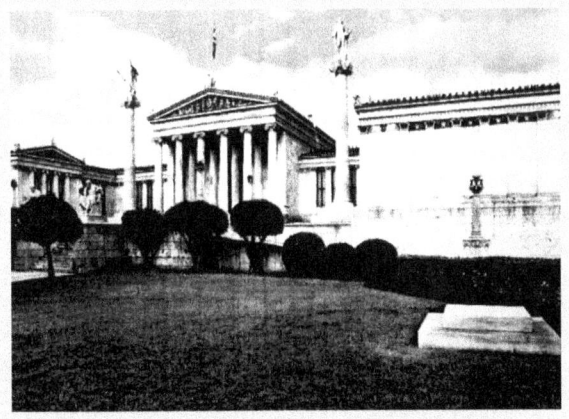

Natasa Biza
Paroikia, Paros
84 400, Cyclades

Professor James Wright
Director of American School of Classical Studies at Athens
54 Souidias Street
106 76, Athens

May 8, 2014

Dear Prof. Wright,

I recently visited the archaeological site of the Athenian Agora and I am writing to you to address a question concerning the flora of the site, which occurred to me after I read the booklet *Garden Lore of Ancient Athens*, published by the American School. The writers of the booklet mention:

"[…] since the excavation of the Athenian Agora has uncovered evidence for planting, the area has been replanted, **in an attempt to give something of its ancient aspect to the visitor, with trees and shrubs of the sort that grew there in antiquity.**" (p.4)

The sign at the entrance of the site also mentions that "[...] systematic excavations in the area, followed by the planting of the trees during the 1950's .**Native plants which were already known in ancient Greece, were chosen for the planting.**"

As I walked around the site, however, I noticed that several of the plants there currently neither are, nor were indigenous to Greece. They were imported later.

Here follow some examples:

Euonymus japonicus– Japanese spindle (Japan-China)
Thujaoccidentalis – American Arbor Vitae (North America)
Eucalyptus globulus – Eucalyptus (Tasmania, Australia)
Washingtoniafilifera– California fan Palm (North America)
Pittosporumtobira– Japanese pittosporum (Japan, China, Korea)
Ailanthus Altissima– Tree of Heaven (China, Taiwan)

I hope you find this information useful, and look forward to your opinion.

Thanking you for your time

Yours sincerely,
Natasa Biza

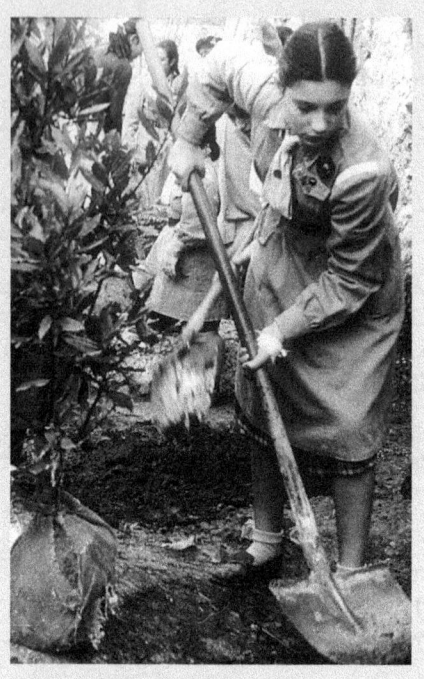

Archive Number: 2008.18.0247
  Title: Girl Guide planting a laurel tree, December 12, 1954
Negative: HAT 54-507
  Date: 12 Dec 1954
Bibliography: Mauzy (2006), p. 103, fig. 227.
    Rating: 4

www.agathe.gr

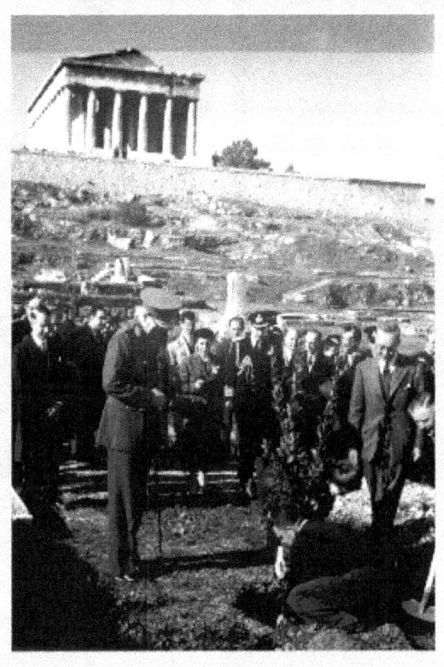

Archive Number: 2004.01.1249
    Title: Landscaping of the Agora. King Paul is planting an
        oak tree. At right, the Director John L. Caskey.
    Negative: HAT 54-33
Personal Name: Paul, King of the Hellenes / John L. Caskey
    Date: 4 Jan 1954
    Rating: 1

www.agathe.gr

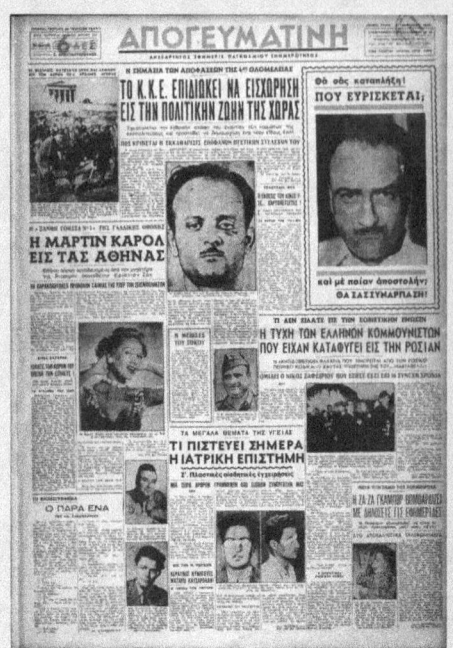
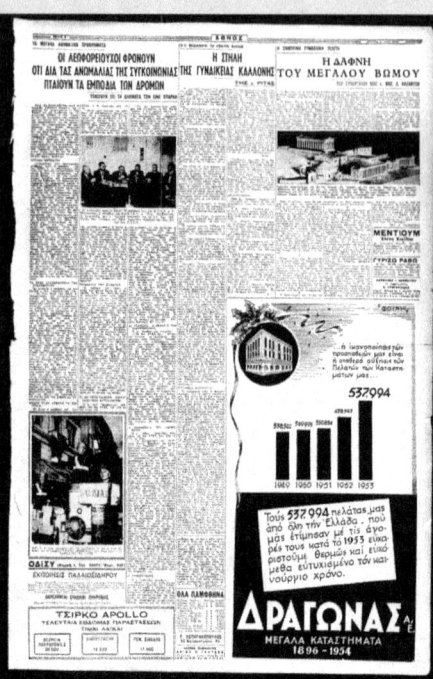
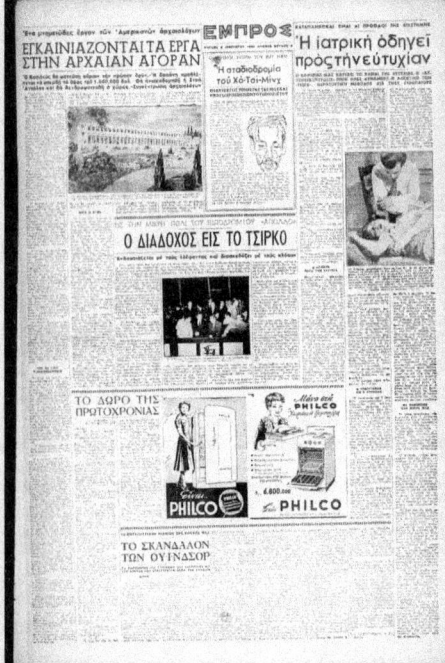
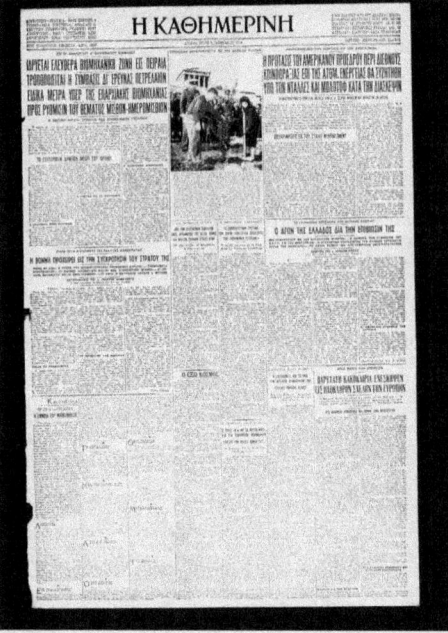

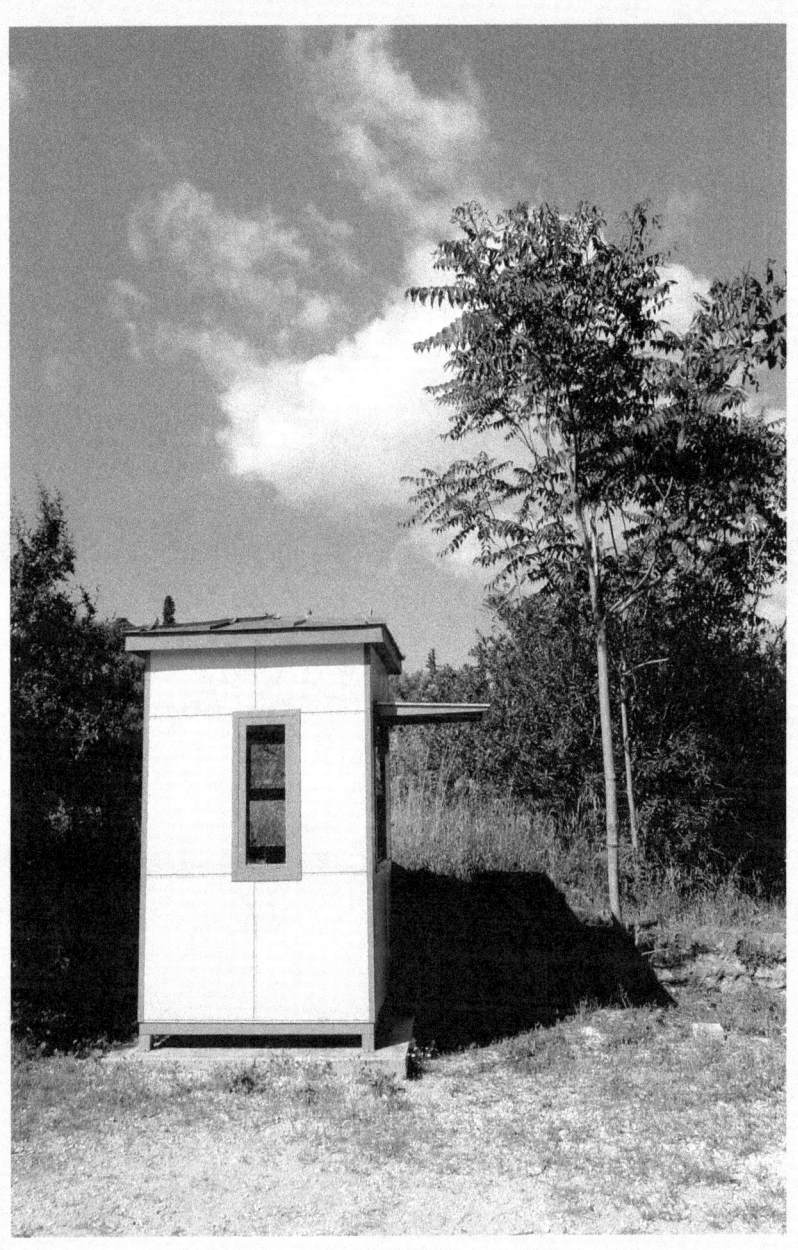

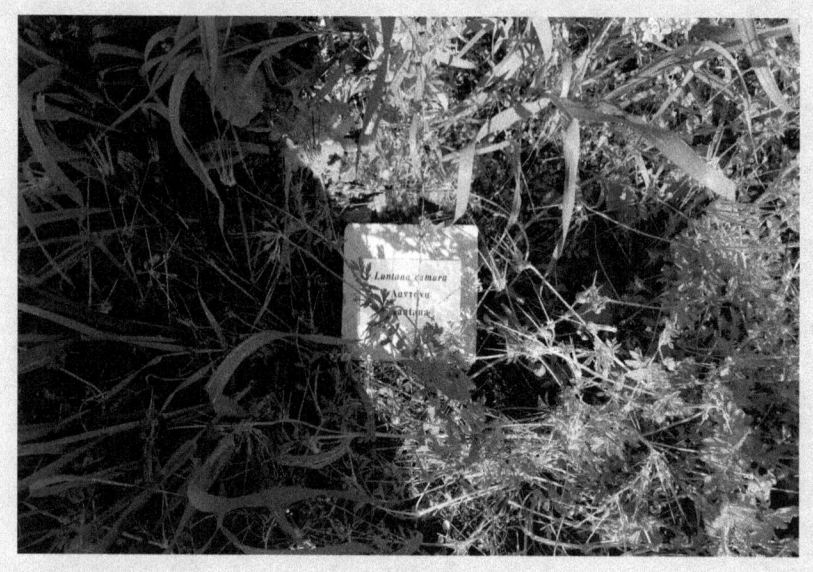

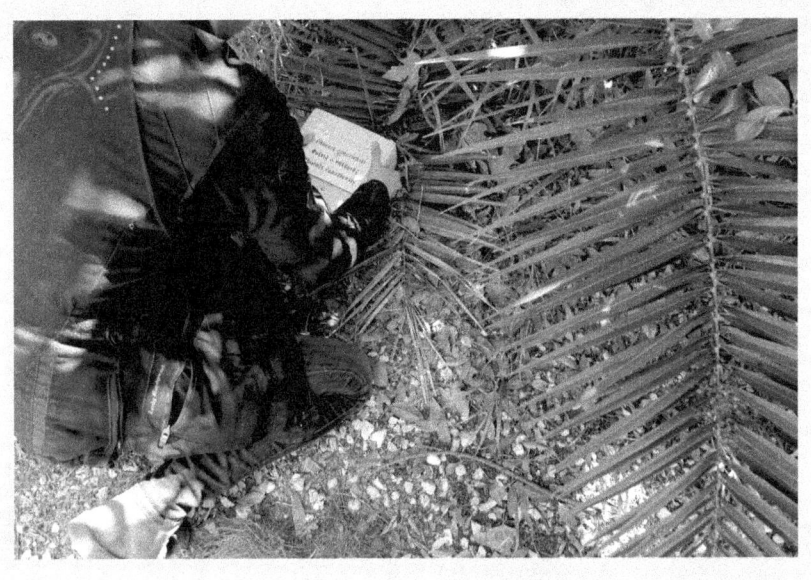

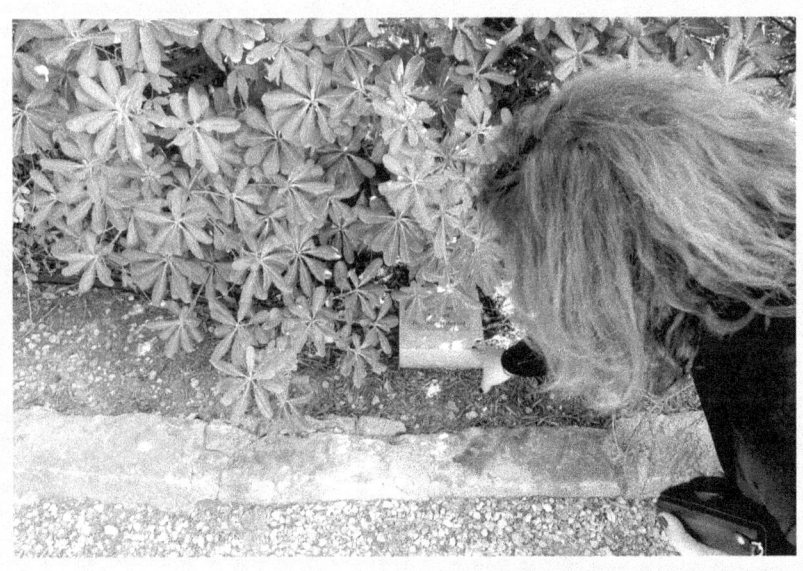

Rerouted and Disordered
Umgeleitete Erzählungen

A Narrative Investigation
On Backgrounds and Background Listening

Amazons in Amazonia
The Loa is a literary form that emerged around 1700: One of the many cultural blossoms of the Siglo de Oro – the Golden Age – gilded by the exploitation of the so called Americas. By inventing the Loa the actors introduced introducing themself as part of the theatre piece. Another part of this newly invented form would be also to mock their patrons and point out financial dependencies. Travelling theatres very often had several Loas which they adjusted to local circumstances. The beginning of this introduction to a new series of work is situated in that time, which was the Loa's time, hijacked by a group of women with different backgrounds and several genders. To reach a fluent narration the Orinoco River is being redirected into the Amazonas. Marie Høeg dumps Bolette Berg on their journey looking for Amazons in Amazonia. Discussing today's gender mainstreaming in real politics and art institutions, missled by a fantastic description of where and how to find the Amazons.

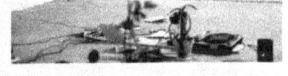

LOA – An Introduction (souterrain Zurich September 10th 2014)

What democracy and for whom?
Marie Høeg and Bolette Berg continue their journey to a record store opening that day. Shortly after giving her famous speech for women's rights to vote in her studio in Horten, Marie Høeg takes a break at the North Pole posing as Fridtjof Nansen. The story loses its protagonists drifting along the chapters of the record store. In addition, the performance picks up key words from actual political debates about migration laws, work migration and women as a recently rediscovered idle economic resource, as well as subcultural movements, music titles and quotes by she DJs. The performance uses the associative potential of languages to construct a fragmented multi-layered story that breaks with chronology by using figures across times in the same way that quotes can be used.

trans-atlantic feedback

I like the tone of this place (OOR Zurich September 14th 2014)

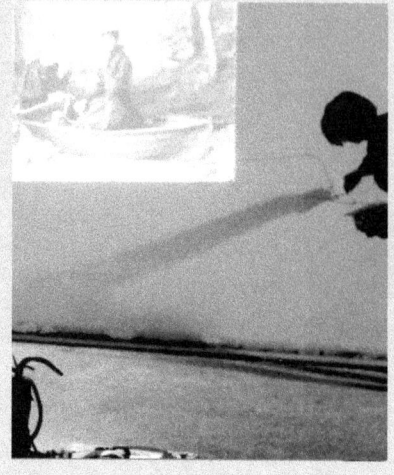

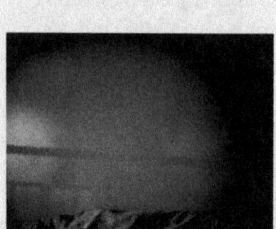

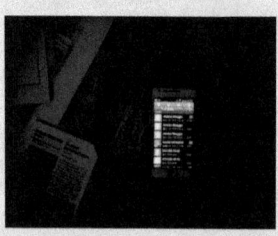

**Backgrounds
Background Listening
Points of Access
Points of Entrance
Vigilance
Embodiment
Unlearn & Forget
It's Time, it's Time for That Again!
Silence is a Powerful Antidote?
Dropping in or
Dropping out:**

Colonies of the Bourgeosie

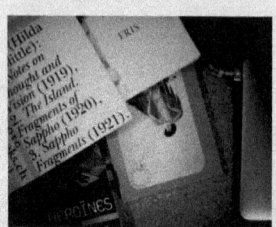

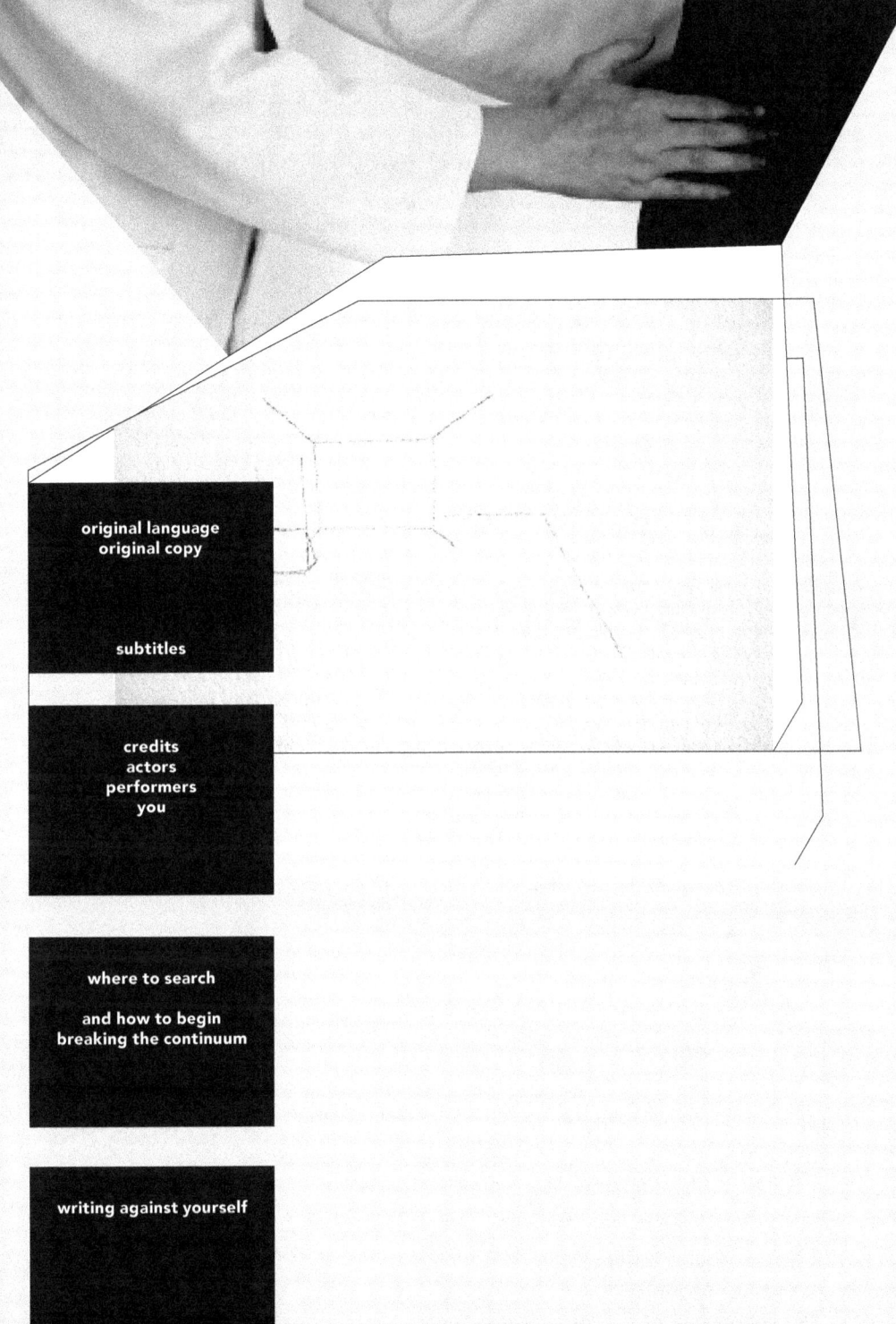

original language
original copy

subtitles

credits
actors
performers
you

where to search

and how to begin
breaking the continuum

writing against yourself

Digging. Not like an archeologist of the 19th Century. Rather like a writer that goes from one association to an other, following the tone of a word, the sound of that voice.

Europe around 1900.
Artists. Bourgeoisie.
The daughters of the factory owners, not the workers in the factories.

Fragments of Sappho
Hilda Doolittle, 1921

*Where does the body come inn?
What is the body?*

There is her strength – Sappho of Mytilene was a Greek. And in all her ecstasies, her burnings, her Asiatic riot of colour, her cry to that Phoenicien deity, „Adonis, Adonis" – her phrases, so simple yet in any but her hands in danger of overpowering sensuousness, her touches of Oriental realism, „purple napkins" and „soft cushions" are yet tempered, moderated by a craft never surpassed in literature. The beauty of Aphrodite it is true is the constant, reiterated subject of her singing.

Orphée of the Quat-z-arts
Florine Stettheimer (in a white modernistic rope),
Crystal Flowers, 1912

*To the right of the stage, are seen the lights of the restaurant „Les Ambassadeurs."
Orpheus dances, his followers take up the dance and it becomes a wild baccanalia.*

Sappho the Missunderstood
Claude Cahun, Héroïnes, 1925

All the people, amassed on the beach, saw me above, at once immense andminuscule, at the tip of the fatal rock.—I'm no fool! It was only a mannequinof hers that Cleis, hidden, pushed into the violet sea. (They do the same thing in the movies.) Atthis has good ears: Did she not hear my cry of agony as Ismashed against the reefs?

Alas! the soothsayers have assured me that my womb is sterile. —Sterile? It's possible, but not for sure. How to prove it with such lovers?

Inverted Odyssees

„They would go through Hellas too. To manifest who they were, that their history was long and given. Using these figures as costumes."

„Even when wearing costumes, they not only reveal their many selves but also uncover an evolving, more fluid concept of identity."

Europe around 2000.
Artists. Bourgeoisie.
The daughters of the bourgeoisie.

Browsing the Underground, September 25 2014

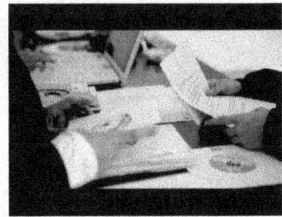

„Can you help me? I forgot something here after my performance."

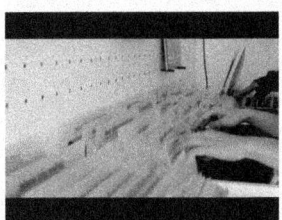

„And then there is an other task: I am trying to find the Greeks inside of me. In a conversational way rather than in a discursive one."

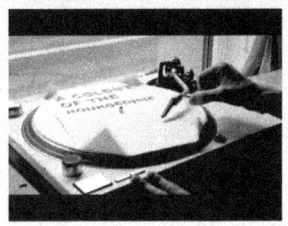

„Let's consider what is internalized: this Colony of the Bourgeoisie: is it very loud?"

Searching the Basement, September 26 2014

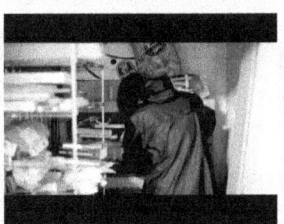

„Nothing. All thrown away. That part of higher education. All thrown away. But unlearned?"

Consulting my Sister the Gyneologist, September 27 2014

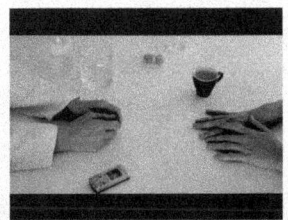

„So what is it about today?"

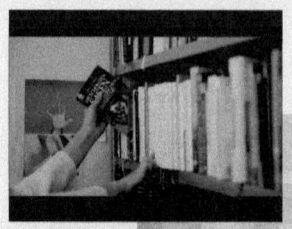

„Today it is not about knowing all the Greek Mythology anymore to mark the affiliation to certain class and taste."

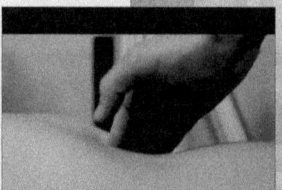

„It is very difficult to locate where and how cultural values get reproduced."

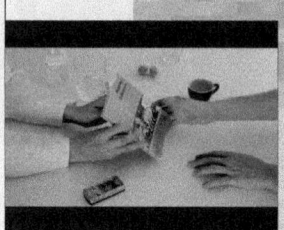

„I could recomend you considering what Claude Cahun wrote about *writing against oneself.*"

„Is that still part of your script?"

On Site Specific Writing

The situation is the stage.
What if there is no situation?

Writing against Oneself

ackgrounds : Within? Internalized?

reen countryside, brown cows along the street.
) minutes by bike 7 o'clock in the morning to go read the
reeks.
o you know how a sleeping cow looks like in winter time
hen it is pitch-dark in the morning and you bike?
) minutes by bike back home to digest the Greeks.
riginal texts in original tongue. Cheating and Lying.
hen translating these classical texts the most exciting
arts about sexuality had been cut out.

/riting against oneself : A practice of unlearning?

igging. Digging like an archeologist?
will never finish lifting up all these faces. Claud Cahun
ıys. Digging for wishes and dreams that are named for
ıshes and dreams. Waiting to be awakened, to find a form
 be shared.
hat have the old Greeks got to do in here, now that
e don't use their names anymore to name wishes and
reams?

Background Listening

Overtitles

Unoriginal Languages

Subtitles

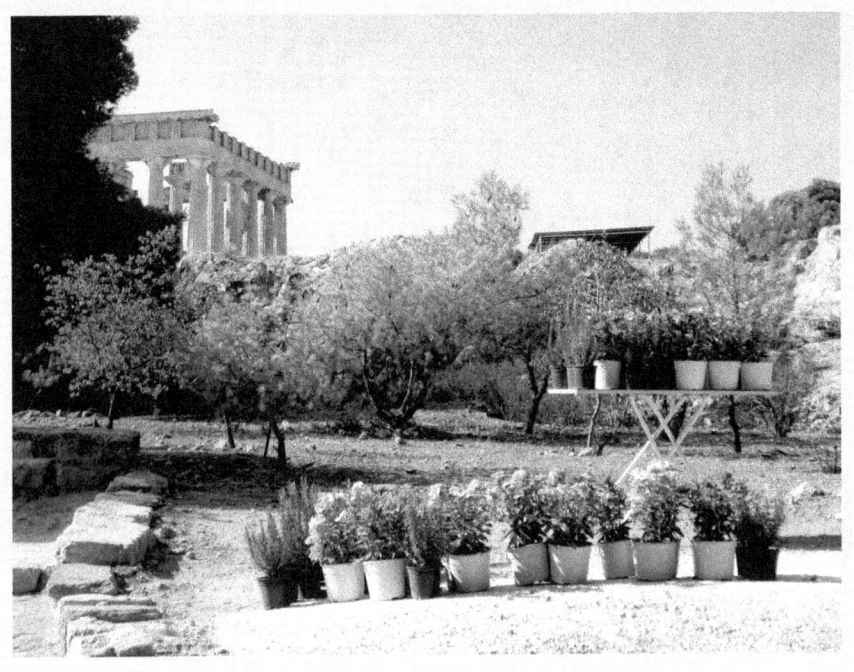

Minor Alterations of Legal Texts or other Regulations - Selling Flowers at the Aphaia Temple

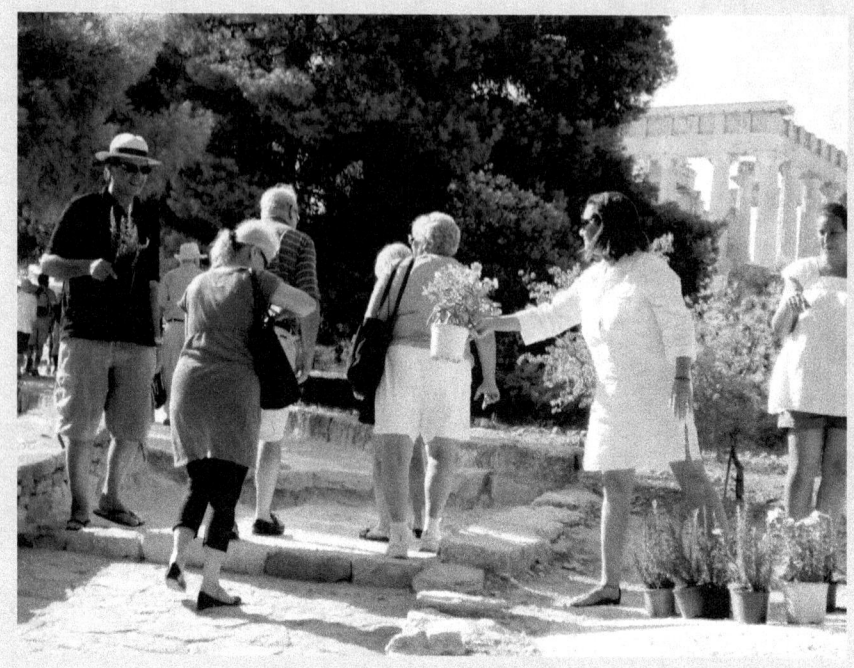

Converting, re-organizing urban conditions and transforming urban reality into a new unfamiliar environment.

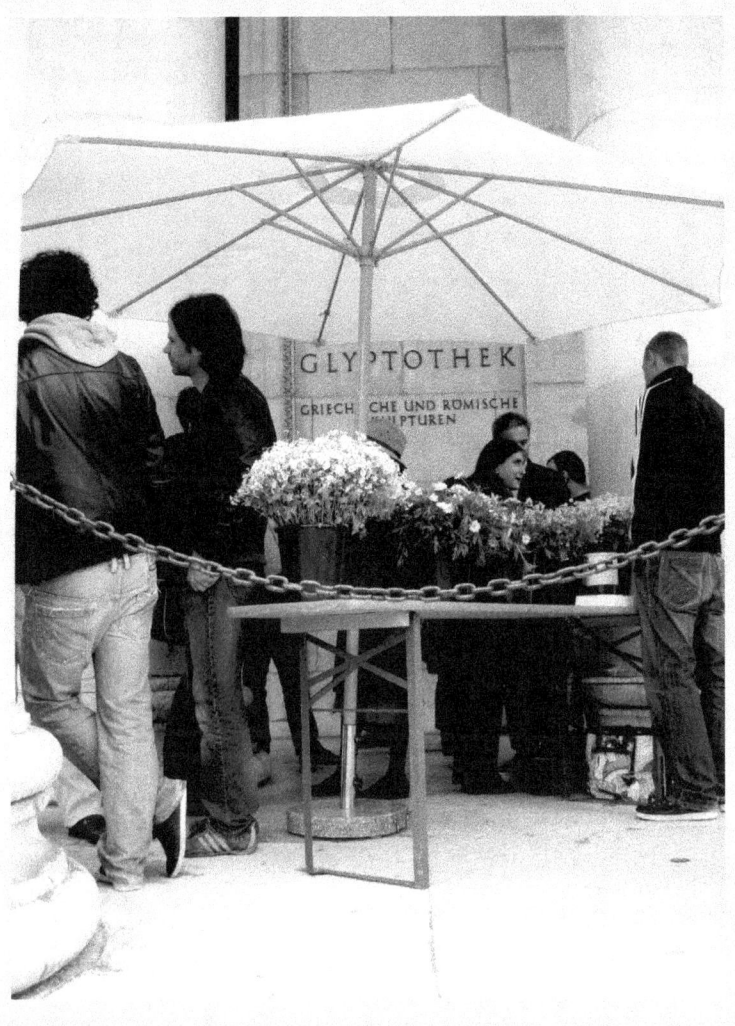

Minor Alterations of Legal Texts or other Regulations - Selling Folwers at the Glyptothek

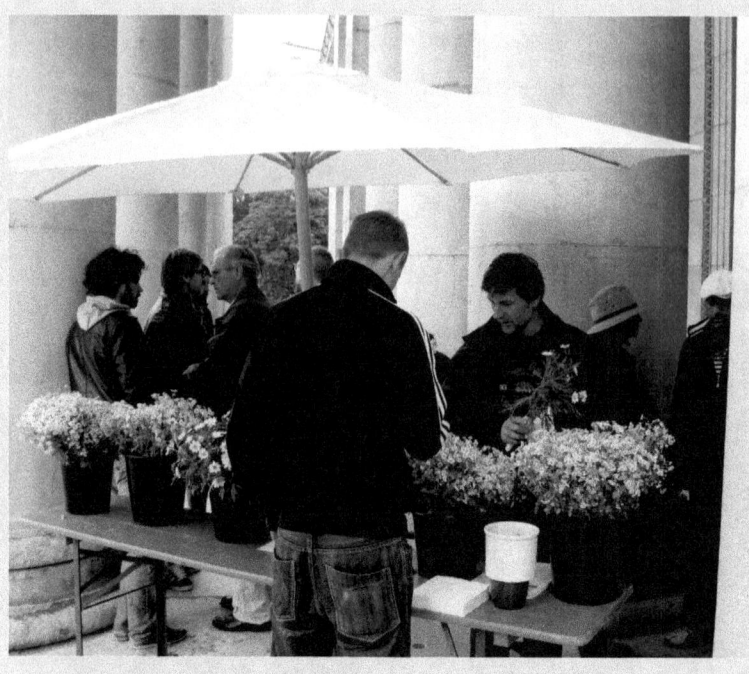

Establishing an alternative but at the same time direct connection between antiquity and present.

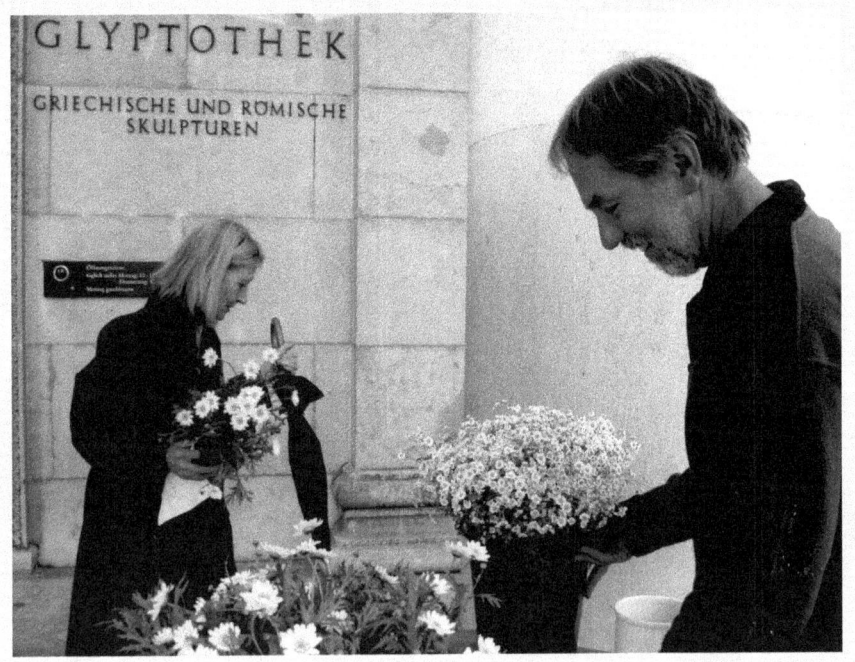

Creating a vibrant, informal situation to produce a contrast to the various meanings of the two institutions.

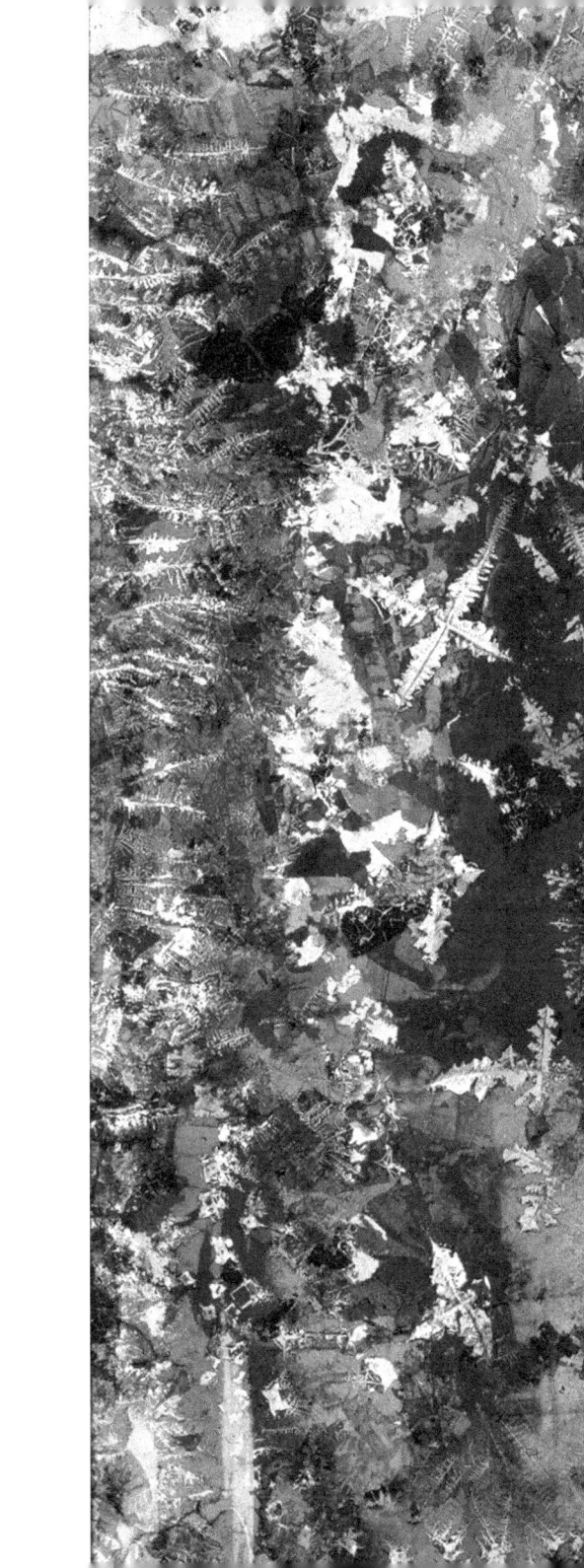

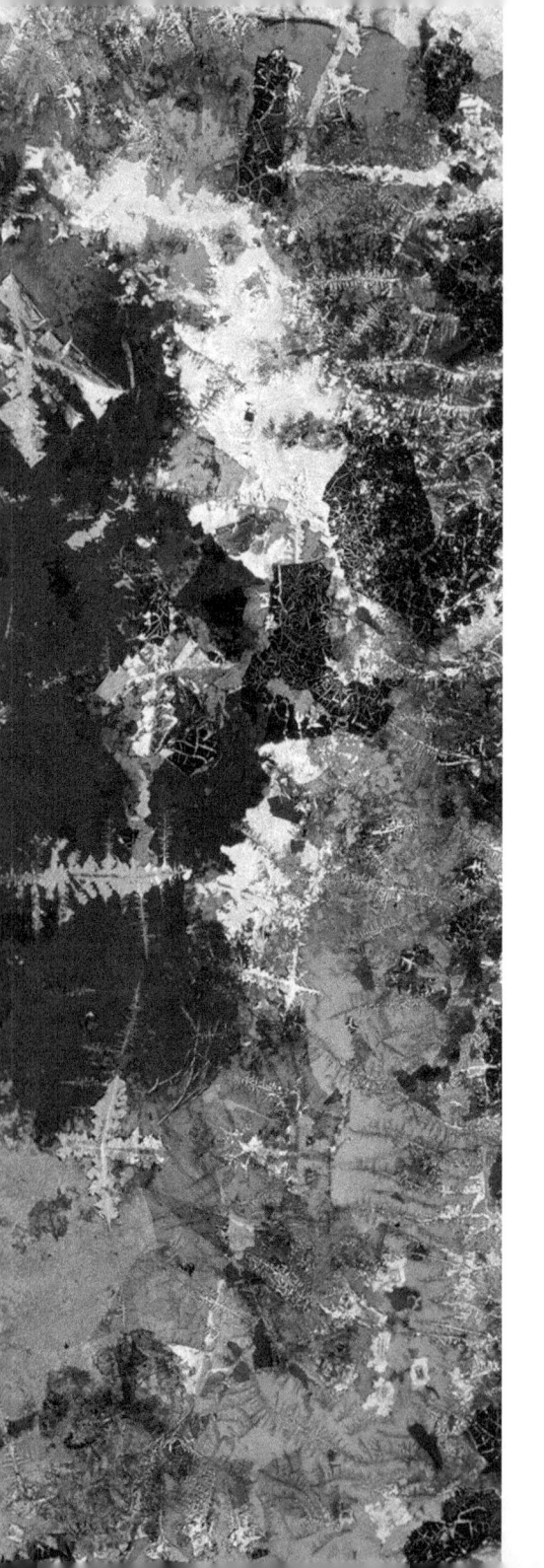

Of Roots and Cultures

What seeds are sown and which ones take root in any given place? How do plants spread and which soil is ready to accept them? What ideological constructs distinguish the "native" from the "imported", the "self-sown" from the "cultivated", the "weed" from the "flower"? These are some of the questions raised in the artwork, A Plan for Planting by Natasa Biza, which echoes themes present in some of her earlier work grappling with the power of institutions, the fragility of social relationships, and the politics of collecting and archiving. In addition to these issues, however, in her current work Biza raises questions more familiar to Greek history and society, highlighting the paradoxes that arise out of the national and international significance of the ancient Greek classical heritage, as well as the politics of memory and oblivion accompanying the national search for "roots" and "continuities" in time and place.

The starting point for this work is a landscaping project undertaken in the mid-twentieth century, organized by the American School of Classical Studies and involving the planting of the ancient Athenian Agora with native species that had grown there in antiquity. This particular School – one of several foreign archaeological institutions in Greece – had staked its claim to the excavation rights in respect of this ancient site after putting pressure on the Greek government in what was an economically and politically difficult period of Greek history and had been working on the site ever since the 1920s (Σακκά 2002, Sakka 2008, Hamilakis 2013). Following the excavation, the School also set itself the goal of reconstituting the archaeological landscape in general terms, not just through the reconstruction of monuments such as the Stoa of Attalos (Sakka 2013), but also by "restoring" the ancient flora of Attica (see Loukaki 2008).

Today, nearly a century later, visitors can walk about this archaeological site and read the names of the ancient Greek plants inscribed on labels set in the ground. Nevertheless, these plants are part of a wider "community of plants", many of which remain anonymous: plants that are not indigenous and did not exist in antiquity, but "migrated" to Greece many centuries later, spread by birds, or carried on the air, or through human intervention. Biza's visual art seeks to name these "out of place" plants, giving them an identity and presence.

Having made tags similar to the existing ones, she engraved on them the names of these "immigrant plants" and placed them at their base. Her intervention on the archaeological site itself was accompanied by a similar intervention in the small guide book available at the museum shop outlining the history of the landscaping project (Thompson & Griswold 1963). Just as she attempts to "fill in" the names of the "anonymous" plants that are absent from the official narrative of the archaeological trail, she adds images and texts from the history of the replanting to the booklet, thus intervening in the dominant narrative and highlighting its "silences". Her final visual installation is based on the mapping of these actions, as well as on an exhibit of archival photographs capturing moments of the replanting process, carried out with the help of boy scouts, archaeologists, Athenians and Americans, as well as the then king and queen. Thus she reveals the political, local and national aspects, as well as the international scope of the task of the original planting. Finally, the installation includes the letter Biza sent to the current Director of the American School of Classical Studies inquiring about his position on the landscaping project.

Biza's art project appears at first to target the "(crypto-) colonial" gaze of the West over Greek antiquity (Herzfeld 2002), which (re)constructs the Hellenic topos (Leontis 1995) and with it the Greek national past and present. Nevertheless, the landscaping project and the logic driving it emerged not just from the research and aesthetic pursuits of one specific Archaeological School, but also from certain national trends, aspirations and feelings of nostalgia in Greece that supported this project.

From as far back as the early nineteenth century under the influence of Bavarian neoclassicism, the newly formed Greek nation had been looking for its neohellenic roots in its classical ancestry. The Greek land became a reference point in the effort to prove and showcase the autochthony, "continuity", and "revival" of the Greek nation (see Σκοπετέα 1988). Archaeological excavations and archaeology in general constituted a national and patriotic project, signifying the rebirth of a nation which had been buried for centuries. At the same time, the renovation and restoration of ancient Greek monuments (Μαλλούχου-Tufano 1998) and the reconstruction of archaeological sites as a whole, came to signify the actual process of building the Greek nation-state which was attempting the reterritorialisation of ancient Greek glory and with it Greece's place in the modern world (Yalouri 2001). Under this regime, both monuments and sites which for centuries had been part of the "social time" of everyday life (Herzfeld 1991), were fenced in and "purified" of anything incompatible with the dominant Greek national narrative, so that they could be declared "ancient sites". It is no coincidence that it was for the specific purpose of allowing the American School of Classical Studies to carry out their archaeological excavations of the Agora, that the old district of Vlasarou had to be demolished causing many residents to lose their homes in – as archaeologists and politicians of the time claimed –the "national interest".

The relationship between land or landscape, territory and nation is nothing new, nor does it apply only to Greece. The conflation of peoples with "national homelands" becomes systematically visible through botanical metaphors of everyday language, such as those that liken the nation to a large family tree rooted in "the nourishing home soil". This naturalization of the conflation between people and land leads to the conceptualization of displacement as a pathological condition and is perceived in terms of the "botanical and quasi-ecological" metaphor of uprooting (Malkki 1992).

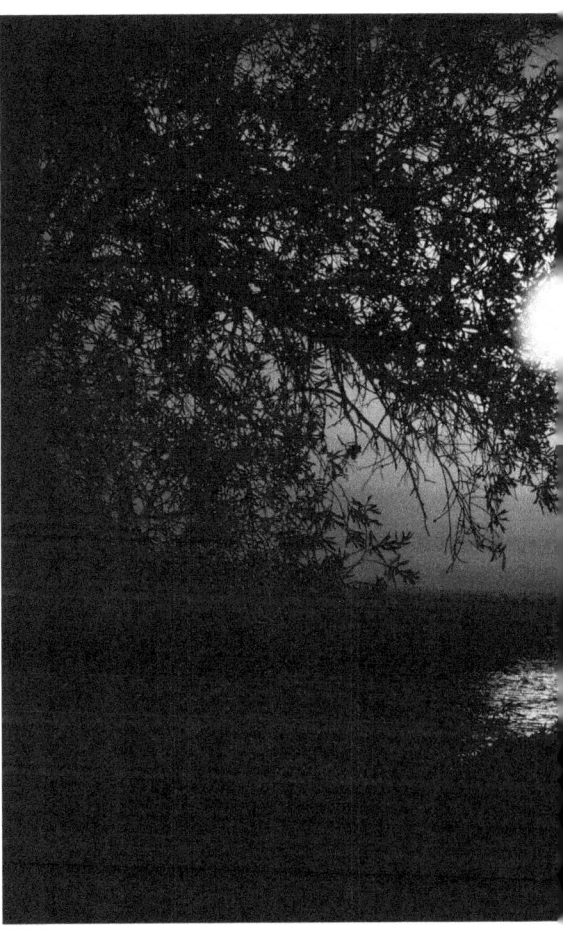

In this context, landscaping choices, and the process of naming certain plants while excluding others are not "innocent" acts. From the 1970s onwards, social anthropologists and other scholars have analyzed the political forces behind the power to name, and the ways in which a "name" can become a tool for the establishment, the rejection and negotiation of identities. Moreover, the relationship between archaeology, names and national identity has been revealed through research in Greece and elsewhere. Abu-El-Haj (1998, 2001), for example, has analyzed the involvement of archaeological projects in the renaming of the Israeli landscape with "real" biblical names, in an attempt to erase Palestinian history from the landscape. Similarly, the use of archaeology to certify the "authenticity" and the "ownership" of the names of "national" sites and monuments is familiar in Greece as illustrated in the case of the well-known conflict over the name of Macedonia (Danforth 1984; 1993; 1995, Karakasidou 1993; 1994, Sutton 1997; 1998), as well as the debate over the name "Elgin marbles" vs "Parthenon marbles" (Yalouri 2001). Names do have ideological significance. They "carve out meaning" and "create a nowhere in places" (De Certeau 1986: 104).

They can even outline (national) territories and (re)write histories (Yalouri 2001). Despite Biza's clear references to key national and international issues, she prefers to frame her work in narratives of personal wanderings that lead rather to a philosophy of gardening (Ζήκα 2012, see Μπιζά 2014) than to a serious polemical confrontation with the current political scene or the politics of the past. And for this reason her work – coherent, polysemous and charming – graciously undermines the foundations of institutions and destabilizes the stereotypes they promote, at the same time creating possibilities for new narratives about our daily lives. In that sense it is deeply political. With her unique „gardening", this visual artist undermines conventions and dominant narratives, plants the seeds of defiance, and cultivates new ground by highlighting the supposedly „minor" forms of life.

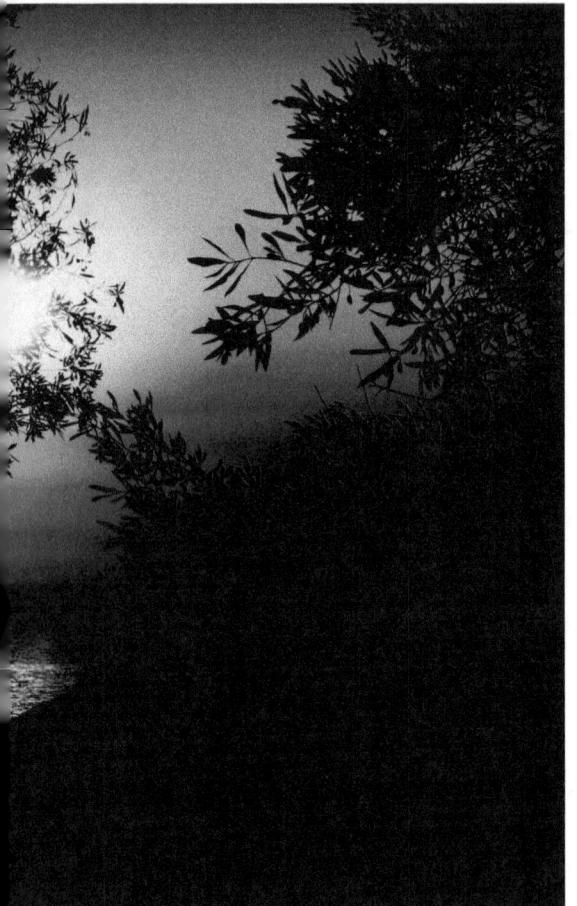

_Elpida Rikou & Eleana Yalouri

References

Abu El-Haj, N. 1998. Translating truths: Nationalism, the practice of archaeology, and the remaking of past and present in contemporary Jerusalem. American Ethnologist 25(2): 166-188.
Abu-El-Haj, N. 2001. Facts on the Ground. University of Chicago Press.
Danforth, L. 1993. Claims to Macedonian Identity, Anthropology Today 9: 3–10.
Danforth, L. 1995. The Macedonian Conflict: Ethnic Nationalism in a Transnational World, Princeton: Princeton University Press.
De Certeau, M. 1986. The Practice of Everyday Life, Berkeley: University of California Press.
Hamilakis, Y. Double Colonization: The Story of the Excavations of the Athenian Agora (1924–1931), Hesperia 82: 153-177.
Herzfeld, M. 1991. A Place in History: Social and Monumental in a Cretan Town, Princeton: Princeton University Press.
Herzfeld, M. 2002. The absent presence: discourses of crypto-colonialism. The South Atlantic Quarterly, 101:4, 899-926.
Karakasidou, A. 1993. Politicizing Culture: Negating Ethnic Identity in Greek Macedonia, Journal of Modern Greek Studies, 11: 1–28.
Karakasidou, A. 1994. Sacred scholars, Profane advocates: Intellectuals molding national conscience in Greece, Identities, 1: 35–62.
Leontis, A. 1995. Topographies of Hellenism: Mapping the Homeland. Ithaca and London: Cornell University Press.
Loukaki, A. 2008. Living Ruins, Value Conflicts. Hampshire and Burlington: Ashgate
Malkki, L. 1992. National Geographic: The rooting of peoples and the territorialization of national identity among scholars and refugees, Cultural Anthropology, 7: 24–44.
Μαλλούχου- Tufano, Φ. 1998. Η Αναστήλωση των Αρχαίων Μνημείων στη Νεώτερη Ελλάδα (1834–1939) [The Restoration of Ancient Monuments in Modern Greece (1834-1939), Athens: Kapon.
Μπιζά, Ν.2014. Σχέδιο Φύτευσης [A Plan for Planting]. MA

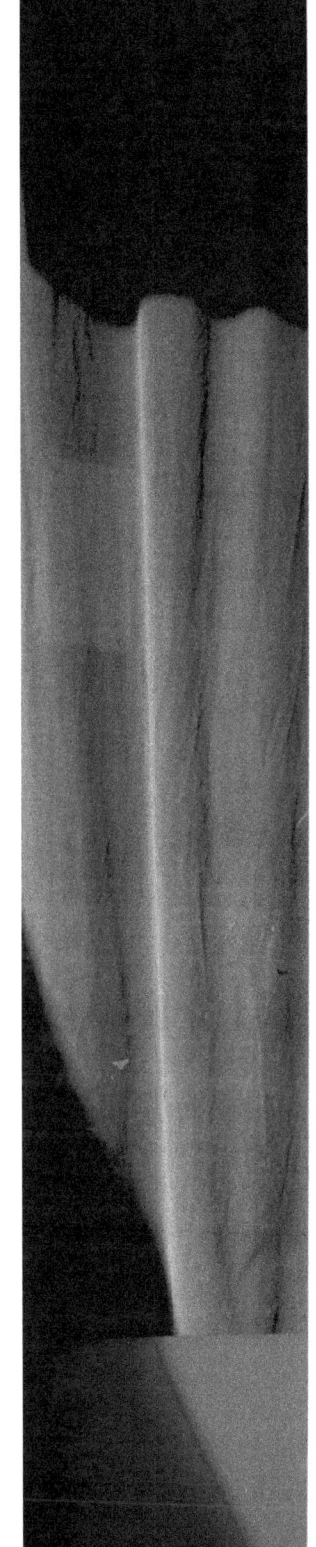

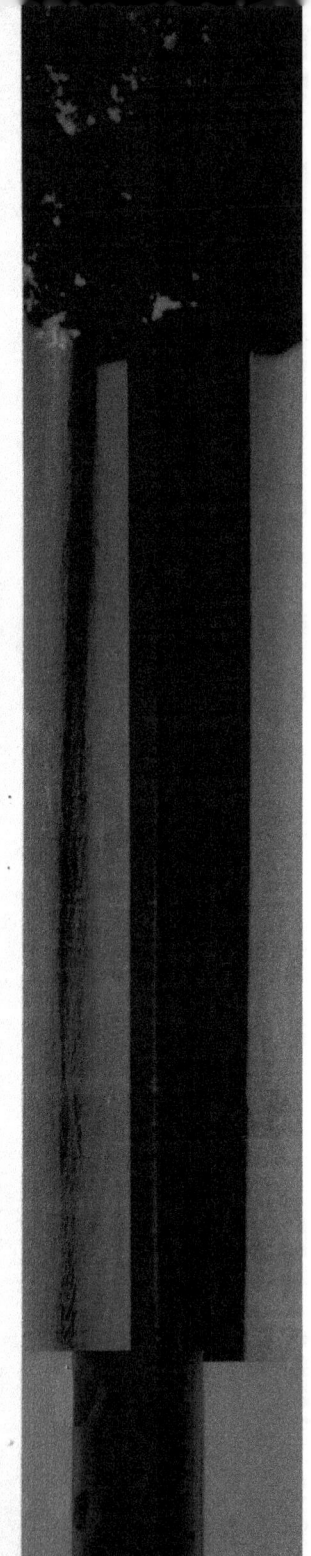

thesis, Athens School of Fine Arts.
Σακκά, Ν. 2002. Αρχαιολογικές Δραστηριότητες στη Νεότερη Ελλάδα (1928-1940). Πολιτικές και Ιδεολογικές Διαστάσεις. Unpublished PhD thesis. Rethymno: University of Crete.
Sakka, N. 2008. The Excavation of the Ancient Agora of Athens: The
Politics of Commissioning and Managing the Project. In D. Damaskos
and D. Plantzos (eds), A Singular Antiquity. Archaeology and Hellenic Identity in Twentieth Century Greece. Athens: Benaki Museum, pp. 111–124.
Sakka, N. 2013. "A Debt to Ancient Wisdom and Beauty": The Reconstruction of the Stoa of Attalos in the Ancient Agora of Athens, Hesperia 82: 203-227.
Σκοπετέα, Ε. 1988. Το Πρότυπο Βασίλειο και η Μεγάλη Ιδέα: Όψεις του Εθνικού Προβλήματος στην Ελλάδα [The Model Kingdom and the Great Idea: Aspects of the National Problem in Greece during 1830–1880], Athens: Polytypo.
Sutton, D.E. 1997. Local names, foreign claims: Family inheritance and national heritage on a Greek island, American Ethnologist, 24 (2): 415–37.
Sutton, D.E. 1998. Memories Cast in Stone: The Relevance of the Past in Everyday Life, Oxford and New York: Berg.
Cambridge, Massachusetts and London: Harvard University Press.
Thompson, D. B. & R. E. Griswold, 1963. Garden Lore of Ancient Athens, Princeton: American School of Classical Studies.
Yalouri, E. 2014. «In the spirit of matter. Re-connecting to antiquity in the Greek present», In D. Tziovas (ed.) Re-imagining the past. Antiquity and Modern Greek Culture, Oxford University Press.
Yalouri, E. 2001. The Acropolis: Global Fame, Local Claim, Oxford: Berg.
Ζήκα, Φ. 2012. Συνάντηση αρχιτεκτονικής και φιλοσοφίας στον κήπο [The meeting of architecture and philosophy at the garden]. In the Proceedings of the conference Η Σημασία της Φιλοσοφίας στην Αρχιτεκτονική Εκπαίδευση [The Significance of Philosophy in Architectural Education], Department of Architecture University of Patras. Athens: Foundation of Panayotis and Efi Miheli.

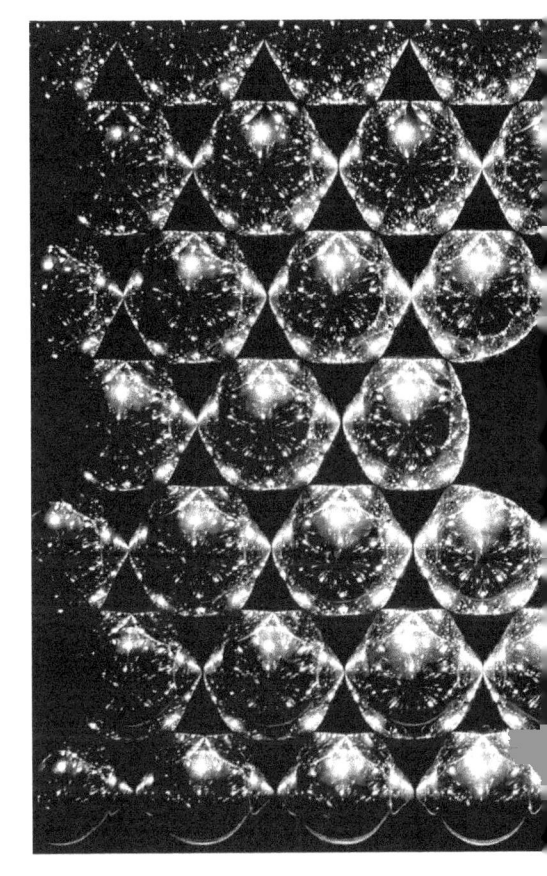

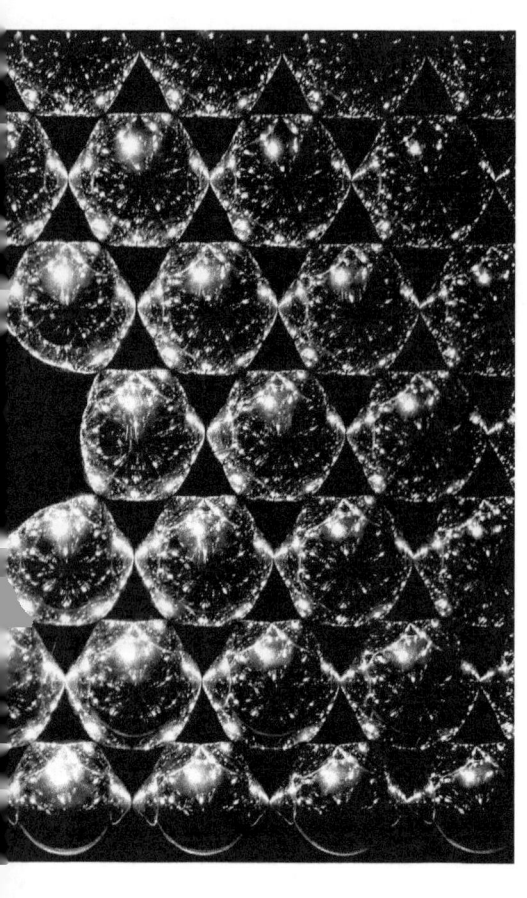

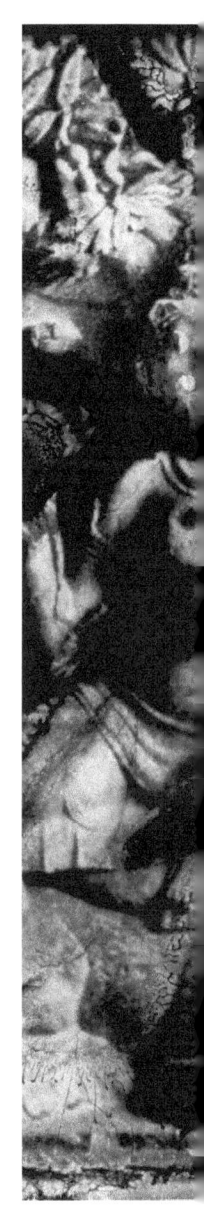

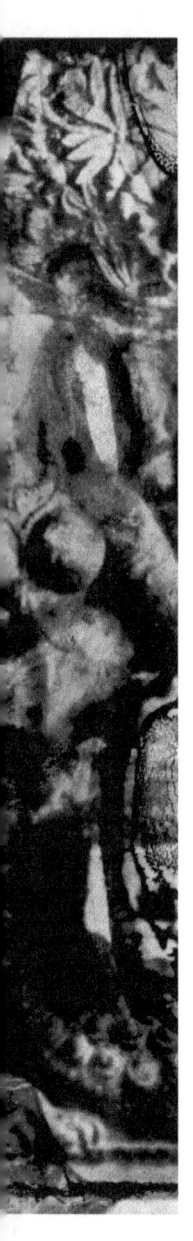

**Evacuating the Political.
New Greek Patriotism in the context of People's Movements.**

The construction of national patriotic imaginaries has always been a primarily concern in the long history of Greece. Like other similar cases of "imagined communities"[1] the Greek nation based its identity on narratives, which have been socially and politically construed for decades or even centuries. Greece has been developing its cultural identity through a constant struggle between eastern and western projections regarding its Ancient, European, Oriental or Balkan affiliations. Alas, when examining in closer detail, in our present time, an emergence of new national imaginaries is still at stake. In the last years of the so called Crisis a new kind of Greek national imaginary seems to gain form. This imaginary grows out of severe considerations on issues such as global financial policies, people's sovereignty and the *governmentality* of the state thereby expressing the need to build up and identify with a new type of contemporary *Greekness*.

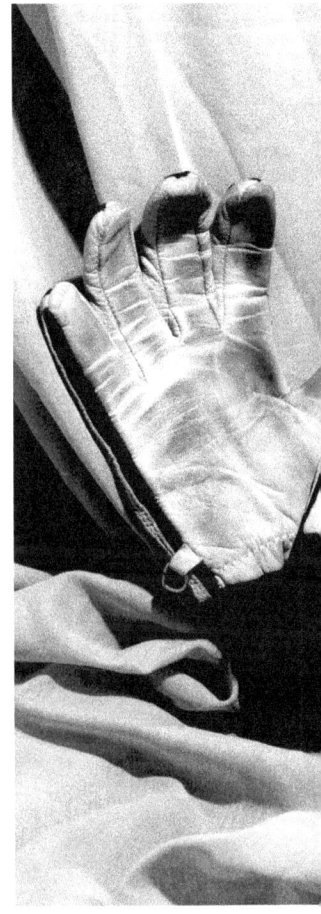

What I am looking to depict within the framework of this essay is the emergence of new kinds of Greek patriotism and their specific origins. Furthermore I will delineate my main concern regarding the notion of the *Political* insofar as this relates to new-fashioned patriotic imaginaries in Greece. In the first instance one can state that these latest patriotic national imaginaries can be seen as a reaction against the current political situation as well as a willful rejection of a political legacy, which is mainly blamed for the ineffectiveness of Greek politics in the previous decades. What counts most for this prevailing construction of a new patriotic identity is the self-/motivation to find ways, individually or collectively for "all Greek people", to resist the effect of political and social decadence over a period of Crisis. This patriotic identity is closely related to people's movements and envisaged by new political parties, which popped up in the period between 2011 and 2014. The latter are therefore willing to establish a new political scenery seen to stand aloof from the old known parties and political organizations.

I must mention alongside my previous point that I am not

---

1 Benedict Anderson, Imagined Communities - Reflections on the Origin and Spread of Nationalism, London: Verso 1991.

advocating that we should disregard all newest forms of political or social mobilization. As a matter of fact there are numerous attempts, or even practices of resistance,[2] which seek to envisage a political confrontation that can challenge the neo-liberal hegemonies of our times. However, I am interested, within the framework of this text, to highlight those political endeavors, which can be related to what I intend to call *Evacuation of the Political*.

Thus I will highlight the political endeavors that focus on a hybrid political constellation that blurs the borders between left, center and right wing politics whilst seeking to produce a new patriotic political identity. This newfound patriotic identity is mainly formed on the basis of a deep rejection of older political parties or even subjects. So the older established party representatives, are mostly seen as "betrayers of the country" or as "Europe's slaves ", who based their political existence more or less on corruption while providing benefits for their own sake. However this doesn't exclude the fact that many of the leaders and members of the new political organizations derived from the established political system of the previous years. Whereas the latter, meaning the political subject, is considered to be an old school idea of a leftist political theory, which doesn't apply anymore. But most important, the ideological division between left, central and right wing politics seems to be no more a criterion for the unity of the patriotic political community. The refreshing patriotic cocktail is now based on a left-central-right wing fusion, which has only one goal: "Save Greece!".

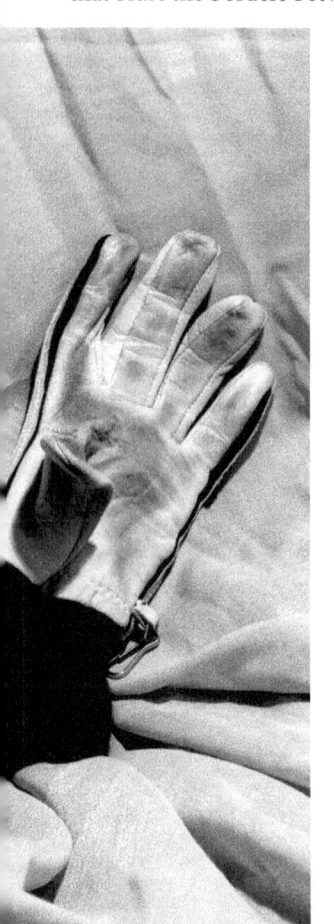

Cut for fun! In some cases political desires speak of the necessity to form a "patriotic front". In other cases the scenarios on the urgency of Greece's sovereignty go so far that one could clearly speak of conspiracy theories and other constructed imaginations regarding geopolitical risks or even "specific threats of forthcoming invasions on Greece's territory".[3] At the same time a common strategy for constructing a strong national feeling

---

2   My purpose is not to neglect categorically all forms of political organization. In the last five years the appearance of political practices or interventions, which deal with social common issues on a local scale (militant research, re-appropriation and re-activation of public spaces, social networks, alternative economies, etc.) seek to envisage new kinds of political subjectivities. From this point of view we can observe their very role in strengthening the local social movement(s).

3   See the views of EPAM (Unitary People's Front) and SPITHA (Movement of Independent Citizens) on geopolitical or strategic matters of State's Sovereignty.

amongst the people is to blame "the enemies of Greece". So this strategy comprises the targeting of specific politicians, who end up being fetishized as the "absolute evil". A hackneyed example regards German Chancellor Angela Merkel being compared to a whole spectrum of *cruel or bad figures* such as Adolf Hitler, a merciless dominatrix or a very strict mother[4] assaulting her children etc. The mainstream media attention on this matter constructs and focuses on the "hard profiles" of politicians as individuals (i.e. Merkel, Jean-Claude Juncker et. al.) by demonizing - instead of analyzing - their specific politics. In any case conspiratorial scenarios as well as the tactical trivialization of politics reduced to glossy entertainment could be framed in the comic or tragic side of such phenomena.

Cut and return! Whereas a significant multiplication of political forces is taking place in Greece and a new generation of political parties and people's movements are arising, one should be rather skeptical of their fundamental principles.
Let us be fairly cautious about this young political imaginary, which opens up the stage for deep patriotic, xenophobic and nationalistic feelings. To be more specific: A closer look on one side of the so called "Anti-Memorandum block" reveals different variations of new Greek patriotism aggregated with popular rhetoric, which derives from different types of political alliances: popular right, patriotic central-left, split ups of social-democrats and the former communist left.[5] The question arises: What is the unifying force amongst these newborn patriotic parties or people's movements?
Apart from the particular differences regarding the definition of their political

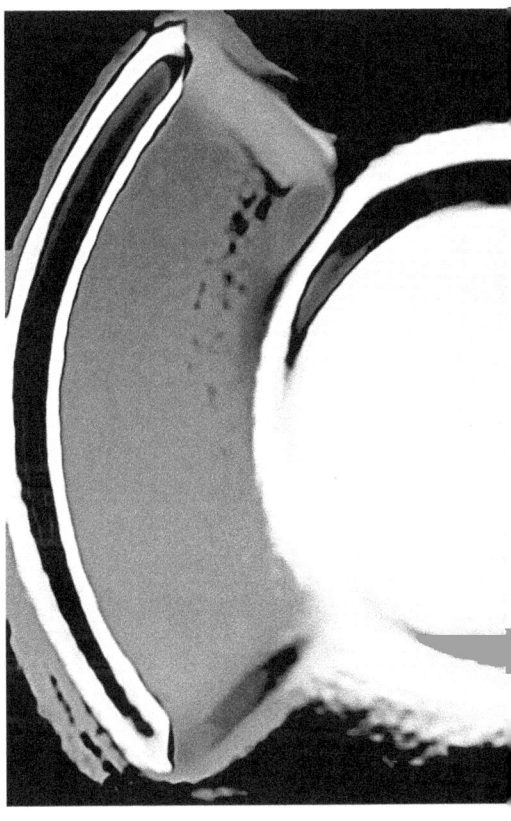

---

4   To be mentioned here: the word "Mutti" (mummy) used in the German Media refers to Angela Merkel.
5   See for Example: Ανεξάρτητοι Έλληνες/ Independent Greeks, Ενιαίο Παλλαϊκό Μέτωπο, Ε.ΠΑ.Μ. / Unitary People's Front (EPAM), ΕΝΩΣΗ ΓΙΑ ΤΗΝ ΠΑΤΡΙΔΑ ΚΑΙ ΤΟΝ ΛΑΟ/ ENOSI GIA TIN PATRIDA KAI TO LAO (Unity for Fatherland and the People), SPITHA Movement of Independent Citizens (recently withdrawn), ΔΡΑΧΜΗ - Ελληνική Δημοκρατική Κίνηση / Drachma - Greek Democratic Movement, et.al.

agenda, many patriotic parties and people's movements state that, Fatherland's unity is the main core objective for their political existence. More or less they all agree that a "patriotic rising" should go along with national independence and people's sovereignty. Their political goal invokes a plea to consider "Fatherland" as the main corpus of people's sovereignty. In that sense ideological distinctions, political backgrounds or even class hierarchies could be overcome for the sake of Greece by focusing on the common patriotic goal. The main unifying force is the desire for a newborn patriotic Greece.

In accordance, one can also ask whether this new national imaginary, which implies a broader Greek patriotic figure to associate and identify with, is well grounded. Let me articulate a hypothesis. The notion of *Greekness*, if there is such a bold synthesis of this, has been shaped through the centuries based on several dispositions and projections. One should also note that the discourse on concepts of Greek´s national identity has grown in strength in the last years of Crisis. In these last years several proposed ways for "entry into" (the global markets/a *success story*) or to "exit from" (the Eurozone, the Crisis) are being represented from different political terrains in order to "save Greece". To propose the best solution for the country's benefit is an on-going task or duty, espcially for the ones who consider themselves as "good patriots". In this context it appears to me that "all patriotic forces are needed now", as stated from different political forces. And it also seems that comparing the extreme right expressions of *national socialism* as in the case of the Golden Dawn all other softer patriotic and nationalist expressions are legitimate. How should we deal with all these different patriotic formations?

What is at stake here is a rather significant aspect, which deals - in my view - with the notion of political conflict. I would like to

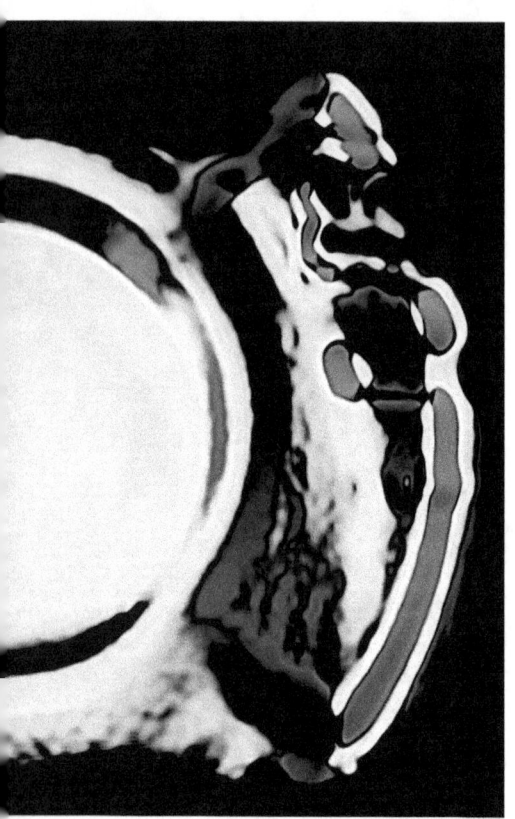

stress that a transformation of the notion of the *Political* [6] is taking place within a bigger scale of the political public sphere in Greece. I argue that the new patriotic political imaginary, introduced as an urgent goal for overcoming the effects of Crisis, has loosened the grasp for the potential of social antagonism in the political field.

The conflict of the political, as is the case of the majority of Greece's political sphere, seems to be "translated" in a very questionable way. Even though the potential conflict inherent in social relations is activated within the Greek political scenery, we can still detect the *Evacuation of the Political* on the level of political practices and institutions. Within the patriotic logic of young political organizations the *political adversaries* are considered as *national enemies* or *betrayers*. Also within this same logic there is not much space left for the Political as an open conflict dimension between different political adversaries. To give an example: The main concern of the patriotic people's political organizations is to stand at the side of the Anti-Memorandum block at all costs. The construction of this block, or even called "front" in some cases, disclaims any ideological differences between left, center and right wing politics as long as the patriotic feeling is kept alive. But also social and political antagonism regarding main divisions of social class is reduced to a level of a national catastrophe. As for the proposed solutions they primarily concentrate on a national level under the motto "from Greeks for Greeks".

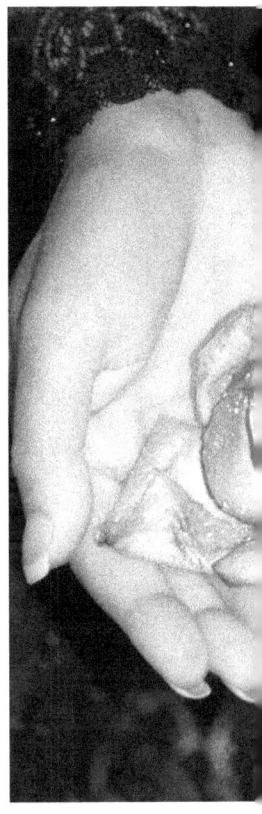

One should not avoid looking more closely to the effects produced by this sort of political understanding. Apparently what we get to experience by approaching these kind of patriotic people's organizations or parties is a blurry image of the Political. But there is more than that. In fact the favored appeal for a unification of all Greeks for the country's sake reduces ant/-agonistic political confrontation into a rally for nationalistic, populist and conservative rhetoric. In this case all different rhetorical strategies aim to dictate the role of the "real patriots". To put it bluntly, this particular view builds on the national imaginary of a heroic Greek figure, who will stand up once again (like their ancient parents did before) and confront all opponents or "enemies", which hinder the prosperity of the beloved fatherland. This is to say that a narrow-minded view of the current political, social and financial situation in Greece reduces the com-

---

6   If we agree with Chantal Mouffe on the fact that the Political is the main dimension of social antagonism, which is constitutive of human societies, we could further claim that Politics should provide the field in which the conflictuality of the political can take shape. Cp. Chantal Mouffe, James Martin (eds.), Hegemony, radical democracy and the political, Abingdon/New York: Routledge 2013, p. 160.

plexity of Crisis and its origins, as seen in a European and also global context.

To come to a conclusion: I am advocating that by transforming the *political adversaries* into *national enemies* one should not expect a lot on the level of democratic politics. In other words, as long as nationalistic and far patriotic feelings intrude into the sphere of political confrontation and open up the space for a holistic dimension of politics there is not much place left for ant-/agonistic political confrontation. Evacuating the Political as in the case of the Greek patriotic scenery means to abandon the terrain of politics in which pluralist or even radical democracy, to borrow Mouffe's political terminology, canoccur.

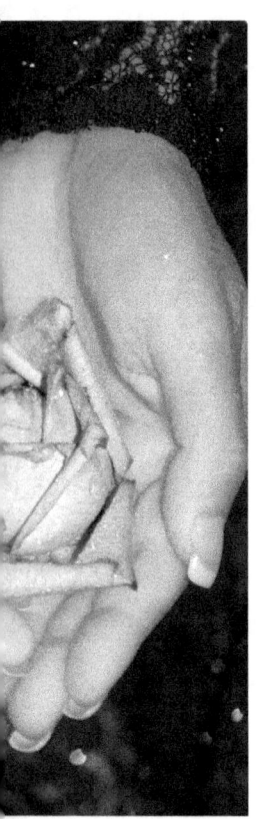

Evacuating the Political is a matter of concern. In my view the transformation of *political adversaries* into *national opponents* cause the following considerations: On the one hand the weakened political distinction between left, center and right wing politics creates no radical confrontation between political adversaries. On the other hand the production of political conflict as seen in the context of parties and people's movements is formed via nationalistic criteria. A main cause of concern is that some political organizations target their alliances (all real Greeks) and opponents (anti-Greeks or non-Greeks) as based on their national integrity. After all the transformation of *political adversaries* into *national enemies* produces distorted political identities and creates a mixed up outcome of far patriotic, nationalistic and conservative expressions. So, for the time being, one can be strongly irritated while watching an upcoming rising of good, bad or ugly patriots.

_Sofia Bempeza

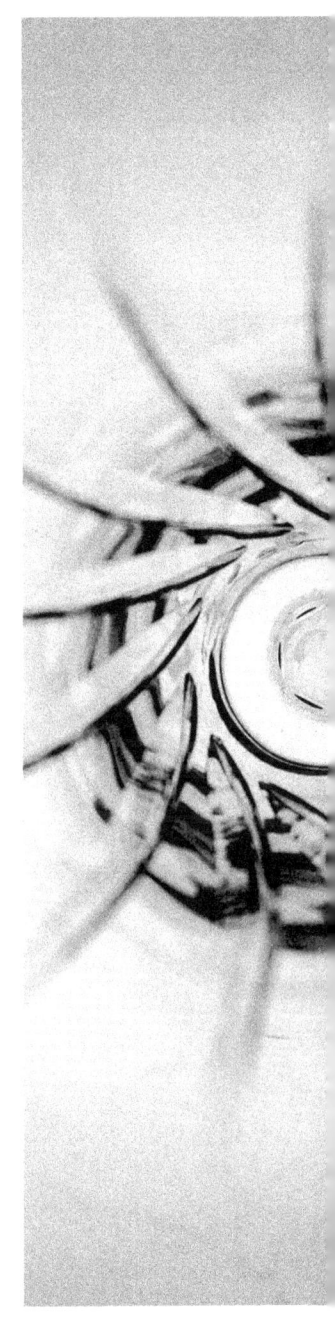

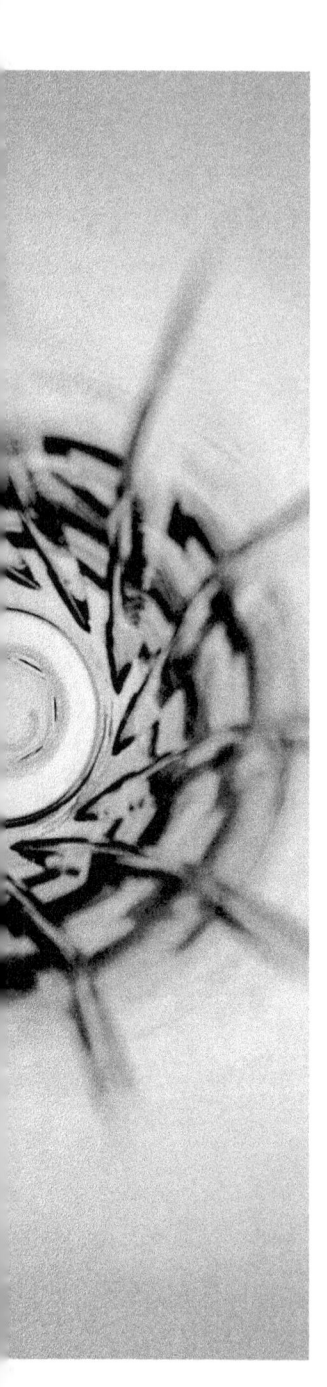

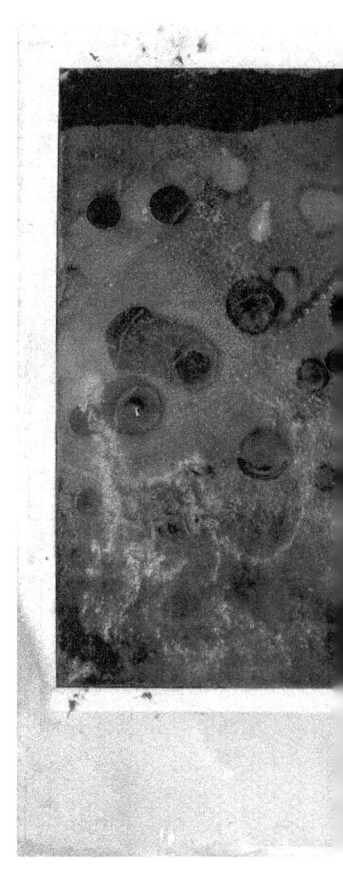

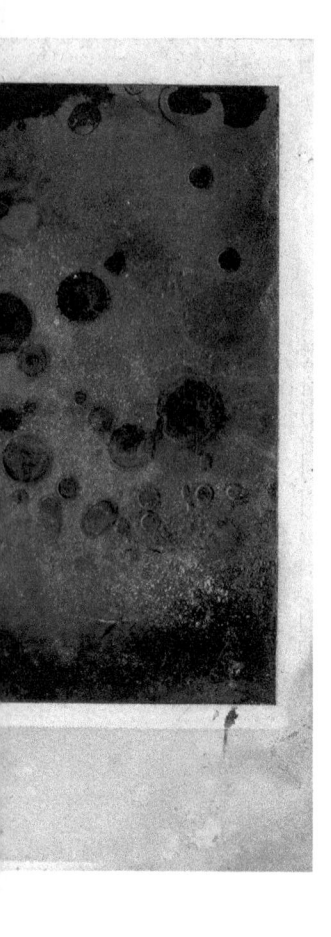

The specter of historical authenticity in today's palingenetic radicalism and the dilemmas of radical art.

Recently, political theorist Nikolas Sevastakis made some insightful remarks on the Scotish referendum for independence held in September 2014. Sevastakis suggested that the supporters for independence cannot be solely viewed as nationalist or anti-English but should also be seen as protesting against the conservatism of English politics and having a strong desire to strengthen Scotland's welfare state. He adds, though, that such a specification is not sufficient for a full-hearted "Yes" vote: 'What is usually ignored or overlooked? The fact, for example, that the idea of separation, as articulated today by various identities in Europe, is coordinated to the overall Eurosceptic cynicism, to an essentially right-wing "regionalism". '[1] Sevastakis views this as a regression to a nationalist communitarianism that fetishizes national community by presenting it as a monopole nodal point for articulating collectivity. The worst part is that this communitarianism annihilates the already diminishing prospect of a European space for liberty, '[…] beyond and above national language, religious or social/class identity […]'.[2]

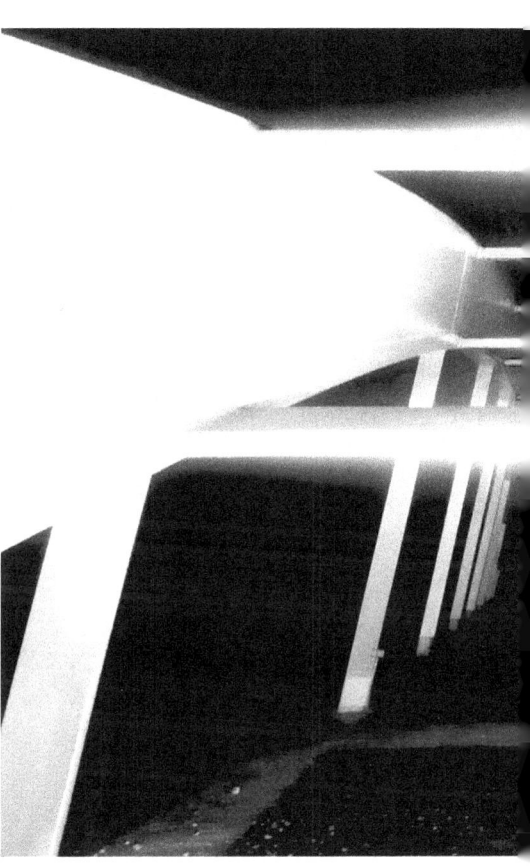

Since the May 2014 European elections, the cooperation between far-right parties and various eurosceptics has become a viable project for the first time in the post-cold war era: a right wing culture of "defense" for the national state against multiculturalism is flirting with a "leftist-reminiscent" rhetoric that devalues Europe as the mouthpiece of the "bureaucrats" and "technocrats" at Brussels. As Vassiliki Georgiadou and Lambrini Rori explain, the European parliament always hosted both the forces of a right wing "nativism" and a

---

1 Nikolas Sevastakis, "Kind intentions and real dangers", Efimerida twn Syntaktwn, 17/09/14, http://www.efsyn.gr/?p=234941
2 Ibid.

left-wing euroscepticism that privileged endogenous (national) development against the "state of Brussels". But, today, as Georgiadou and Rori suggest, the merge slowly taking place is that between the right-wing populist parties and a wide variety of Eurosceptic parties: a new force of "putinism" or "russophilia" seems to convert traditional anti-communists, supra-nationalists and anti-pluralists into admirers of Putin's new authoritarian regime. Various extreme and/or populist right-wing parties seem to foster the Russian agenda: the Greek Golden Dawn and ANEL, the French FN, the German NPD, the Belgian VB, the British BNP, the Italian LN, members of the Hungarian Jobbik, the Bulgarian ATAKA and the Slovakian L'SNS. These forces gradually constitute a front fascinated by the idea of a

a Eurasian Union. This fascination even extends to Nigel Farage's UKIP. [3]

In September 2014, in the same spirit, various Greek parties in the European Parliament (the radical left SYRIZA, the right-wing ANEL, the neo-nazi Golden Dawn and the KKE) voted against the connection between the Ukraine and the E.U. Also some weeks previous, when Putin declared his embargo on the E.U., an elder member of SYRIZA, Manolis Glezos, sent an atavistic letter to Putin, pleading him to exempt Greece from this harsh decision with recognition of the "traditional friendship" between the two countries and of the various historical expressions of Greece's resistance against the plans of the E.U. and the New World Order.[4] As Georgiadou and Rori propose, the understanding of a "putinist" cross front should not reductively focus on the economic crisis and its social effects but should take into account underground ideological processes that, albeit extending to past decades, were not considered important. The influential macho authoritarian political lifestyle of today's

---

3   Vassiliki Georgiadou and Lambrini Rori, "The special magma of anti-europeanism: extreme right-euroscepticists-russophiles", Metarrythmisi, 19/05/14, http://www.metarithmisi.gr/el/readText.asp?textID=30874&sw=1366
4   http://www.naftemporiki.gr/story/840782/m-glezos-epistoli-ston-poutin-gia-arsi-tou-empargko-sta-ellinika-proionta

Russia and the imperialist dreams of a "Eurasian Heartland" are best instantiated by the philosophical political project of the "nazbol" ideologue of Putin's camarilla, Aleksandr Dugin. In his influential "4th Political Theory" (2012), Dugin envisions a spiritualist, environmentalist, traditionalist "new nationalism" with a disposition against particularistic interests and against the fragmentation of identities – a Eurasian nationalist alliance that will militate "atlanticism". This nationalism will be "internationalist" and unitary and will edge against consumerism. It will support local regional identities and oppose the parasitic role of the state enhancing the creation of communities of autarky - a conservative revolution for the 21st Century. [5]

Is this your land? Autonomist politics and regionalism.

In our age, the postmodern wars over the nation, national identity, narration and cultural difference are slowly replaced by a new crux over autonomy, ethnicity and region. Ethnicity, understood as a regional pre-modern identity has become the epicenter for a multitude of claims, some expressing a radicalist definition along the lines of a nuanced (post)national-liberationism (varieties of leftist autonomism) while others openly wish to legitimize a traditionalist narration which justifies the adoration of the past against any change caused by global capitalism (right-wing culturalism).

The discourses that deal with the "regional", traditionalist or de-constructivist, seem to be –more so than ever - loaded with desires, intentions and persuasions. While these desires differ at various levels in respect to their long-term goals, even the most deconstructive of enterprises can suggest that the "great national narrations" should be replaced with the multiple "from below" narrations of individuals and groups – narrations that comprise a cloud of "immediate" and genuine expressions of a nation's (pre)history. Although the emancipatory inspiration of this leftist analysis is distinct from the conservative New Right celebration of the various "ethnies", it often falls prey to calls for "recovering" regional autarky.

Various leftist attacks on the official structure of nationalist narrations often celebrate ideas about the nation as a synthesis of autonomously functional communities that are ready to get rid of the modern devil: the

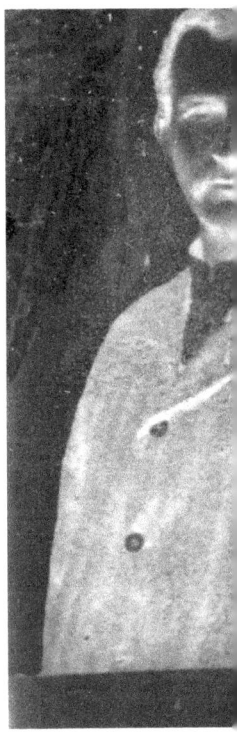

---

5   For research on Dugin's 4th Political Theory visit http://4pt.su

state. This tendency fosters a syncretic "post-Westphalian" myth that can be seen to be influential across various orientations. The autonomist slogan is that the nation should be replaced by a map of collaborating communities without a state regulating the social, cultural and political life. From the writings of the post-situationist left, to autonomous Marxists such as John Holloway, Peter Linebaugh, Silvia Federici, George Caffentzis and Massimo De Angelis, to post-workerists such as Antonio Negri, the processes of "primitive accumulation" are, at various levels, fetishized as the evil side of modernity that slaughtered the wonderful communities of the past (a pretty vague one but sometimes late medieval). When these leftist autonomist discourses attempt to define the "life" of communities beyond the outreach of the modern National State they often seem to be rather unsuccessful in avoiding the idealization of lifestyles as either "authentic", "arbitrary", "perennial" or strictly related to the enjoyment of natural resources (that, "accidentally", are also central to the generic mythology of the National state). Is this a generic feature of autonomist currents or a specific tendency in the work of some thinkers?

A strong aspect in various currents of autonomous Marxism, prompted by a naturalist economist prejudice, is an argument which perceives a certain population as inextricably tied to some land, some material source or "common", as this jargon prefers to mention. By ascribing this "natural" common to a specific population, autonomist theorists latently authenticate various cultural, communal, symbolic practices as sanctified resistance against capitalist accumulation and, thus, ineradicable rootedness. With this line of thought, groups of people are reified via belated cultural differentialism. For example, Peter Linebaugh refers to the prohibition of the use of the Adirondack woods against the native Iroquois Indians from the Forest Preserve in the 1880s:

'to the communities of Iroquois Indians and French Canadians in the Adirondacks, the conservation movement of the 1880s meant "the transformation of previously acceptable practices into illegal acts: hunting or fishing redefined as poaching, foraging as trespassing, the setting of fires as arson, and the cutting of trees as timber theft." These inhabitants were charged by state officials with looking upon the forests as "a piece of commons," or as "a public crib where all may feed who choose." The Forest Commission "endeavored to strike terror, as it was, into the people who trespassed in that way."'[6]

---

6 Peter Linebaugh, The Magna Carta Manifesto: Liberties and Commons for All, Berkeley, University of California Press, 2008, p.3.

At first, something enlightening is offered by this argument: the notion of the "commons", of land as a "common", comes from outside – it is a part of the settler's discourse, the ascription of some habitus. In fact, a quick look at the history of Adirondacks reveals that Adirondacks, the oldest geological formation of North America, has never been a permanent settlement by the two Native American tribes of central New York, the Iroquois and Algonquins. These mountains were mainly visited for hunting and war. In the Iroquois language, „Adirondack" actually means „those who eat trees" and was used to describe the Algonquins that settled to the North.[7] In 1609, a group of French and Algonquins encountered the Iroquois and the French shot their chiefs down. Since then, the Iroquois despised the French and made an alliance with the British. For almost three centuries the region had no inhabitants. In 1885, the state created the Adirondack Forest Preserve and in the 1892 the Adirondack Park was established under constitutional protection.[8] What does this tell us? For sure, the forest preservation policy bereaved natural resources that were accessible to the Iroquois, but the very relation between the Iroquois and the woods had always been contingent and changing rather than permanent and monopolistic. And how does Linebaugh undestand this relation? In a way that overtly essentialises it. He employes an overwhelming metaphor to name all the suppressed labor forces (factory workers, immigrants, slaves) in America that preserved practices of fishing, hunting and horticulture: "the salt of the earth"[9] – something like an organic entity that resides in the soil.

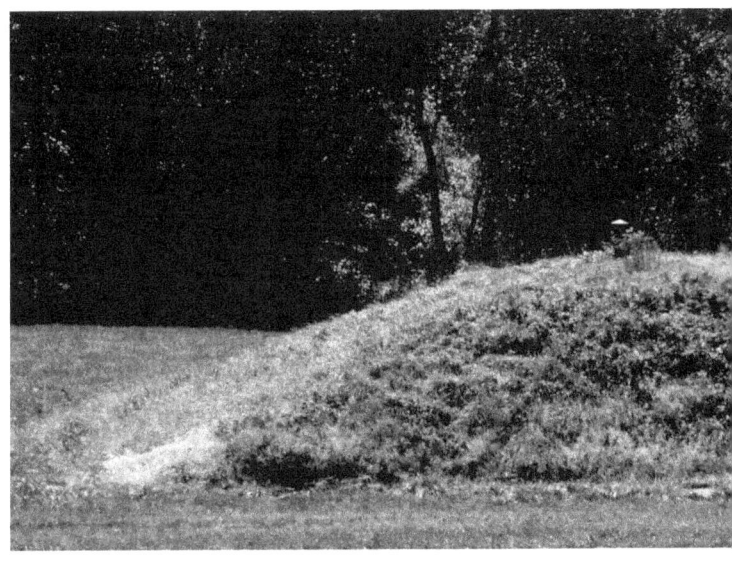

Autonomous Marxists offer important and delicate historical accounts of the processes of capitalist accumulation and their grim consequences. But their emphasis on lost forms of

---

7   http://www.adirondack-park.net/history/adirondacks.html
8   Ibid.
9   Peter Linebaugh, p.243.

of community and practices of "commoning" often leads to the a posteriori construction of an identity as a belated arbitrariness which must be redeemed. And this identity is the promise of the palingenesis of a lost unity between a group and a land that was "free" but now "enclosed". These ideas foster what Ernesto Laclau and Chantal Mouffe have called, in another context, the "naturalist prejudice": an understanding of the "economic" as a limit to society's potential for hegemonic re-composition.[10] A comparison may enlighten the rather languid character of this radicalism: if the old Trotskyist 4th internationalist strategy was to enter the national-liberational movements and turn them into full-blown universalist struggles (a development of the "entryism" thesis after 1951), today's autonomist radicalism is that of a passive pan-collective acceptance of "separation" and dispersal as immanently revolutionary. The means are now identical to the ends.

Palingenetic artistic activism.

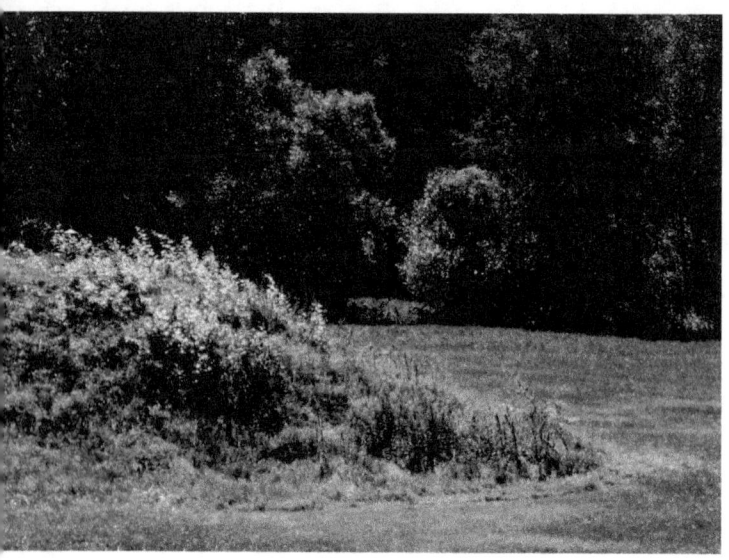

Today's radical dogma is that every internationalist progressive emancipatory struggle is a regional struggle. The facebook page of the New World Summit recently hosted the following post: 'Today the New World Summit added the flag of Scotland to that of its speakers on the front of the Royal Flemish Theater on Brussels. We send our best wishes to the brave campaign of the YES camp: our hopes and hearts for a new world are with you. Yes Scotland!'[11] Of course, the New World Summit is the famous artistic project by Jonas Staal that, since 2012, is in circulation across all biennials and radical art shows. The work started

---

10   Ernesto Laclau & Chantal Mouffe, Hegemony and Socialist Strategy: Towards a Radical Democratic Politics, Verso, London, 2nd edition, 2001, p.70.
11   Last visited on 21/8/2014, https://www.facebook.com/newworldsummit.eu?fref=ts

as an ephemeral-alternative parliament offering its rostrum to representatives of groups, organizations and parties that are blacklisted as terrorists in international "terrorism" lists.[12] Now, the invitees and speakers constitute a wide network of national-liberation movements of various types, ranging from the separatist patriotic left to the separatist nationalist right. Jonas Staal refers to this ensemble as the expression of a legitimate "progressive nationalism" that offers an alternative to the "ultranationalism" of our age. With the term ultranationalism, Staal describes that the nationalist and populist parties plead for deeper, and usually shady, state structures to "protect" the citizens from the "muslim danger" etc. Geert Wilders's Freedom Party in the Netherlands is certainly an exemplary case. Staal wishes to highlight examples of a contemporary progressive nationalism that work in the direction of a "stateless internationalism".[13]

This "progressive nationalism" is exemplified by the recent addition of Natalie McGarry: a pro-independence Scottish political activist and convenor of the Scottish National Party in Glasgow. Her lecture at the Summit was entitled: "The Independence of One, a Victory for Internationalism: Scotland's referendum as the Horizon for Self-Determination in Europe." The idea seems to be rather simple, nothing profound about it: any expression of national/regional independence is the new internationalism. Recently, the Summit hosted Josu Juaristi, a European MP for the Euskal Herria Bildu: a leftwing Basque nationalist and separatist political coalition founded in 2012. Within the coalition one may also find representatives of he wider Ezker Abertzalea (Patriotic Left), the Basque radical nationalist left.[14] In a previous session hosted by the summit, Andoni Lekue, a member of the Basque independence movement presented his idea of the Basque situation

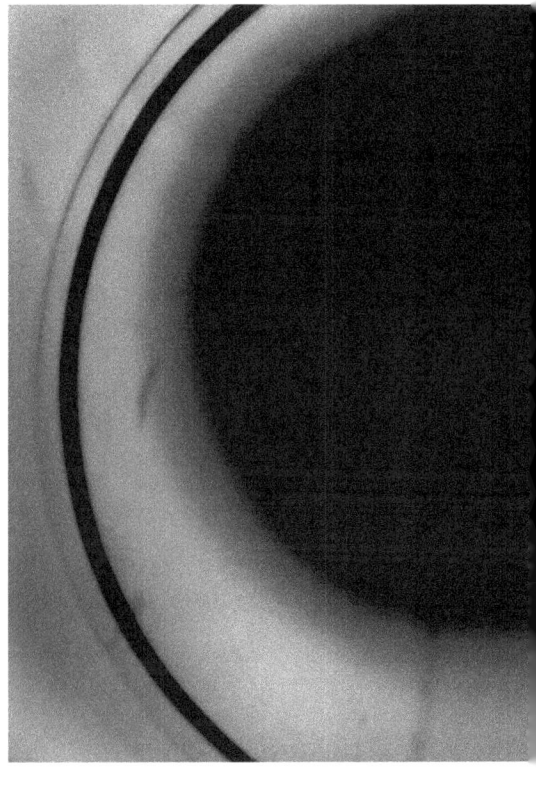

---

12   Visit http://newworldsummit.eu
13   Jonas Staal, "To Make a World, Part I: Ultranationalism and the Art of the Stateless State", at http://www.e-flux.com/journal/to-make-a-world-part-i-ultranationalism-and-the-art-of-the-stateless-state
14   Both representatives are also presented with posts at the New World Summit facebook page, last visited on 21/8/2014, https://www.facebook.com/newworldsummit.eu?fref=ts

as representative of every suppressed subjectivity in the world – a category of civility that supersedes nationality and region.¹⁵ Staal is successful in noticing that this is reminiscent of Subcomandante Marcos's idea of a decentralized Fourth World War that will redeem the numerous annihilated indigenous people of history: "However different the struggles of Marcos, Lekue, and [Fadile] Yıldırım may be, what they share is their defense of a self-determination that, while remaining stateless, is first and foremost a militant cultural struggle. They are the representatives of stateless states—of peoples that precede their administrative representation in the formal, recognized entity of a state."¹⁶

In such statements, a series of radicalist prejudices seem to operate as established universal truths: *At the end of the day, the Basques, or the Kurds will supersede the very idea of the state - their affective identification with other national liberation movements is sufficient in universalizing their struggles.* This is either overtly superficial or ignorant of the history of the many national liberation and Third-wordlist movements since the 1950s. One is also tempted to scratch beneath this abstraction for a civil identity beyond nationality and region as a particular demand by Staal's invitees. The groups, movements and parties invited by Staal share one thing in common: they are paradigmatic, or part, of specific regional separatist struggles. This is the only criterion for entering the alternative parliament that Staal roams around biennials and museums. This common denominator is, indeed, the only truly internationalist aspect of Staal's alternative parliament. What kind of metaphysics lie beneath the fantasy that a separatist coordination against today's ultra-nationalism offers the convergence point for a "better", "progressive" and more open "internationalism"? Is the existence of the National

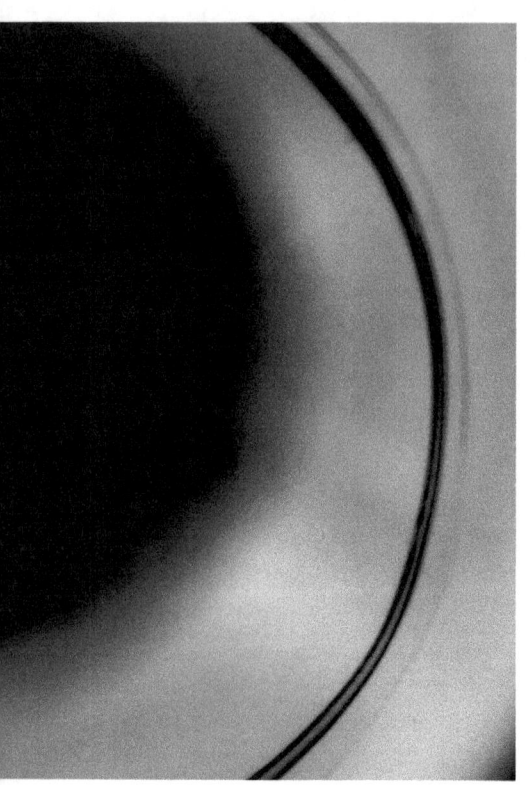

---

15 Jonas Staal, "Art after democratism: the pedagogy of the New World Summit" in Vincent W. J. van Gerven Oei, Adam Staley Groves & Nico Jenkins (eds), Pedagogies of Disaster, The Department of Eagles, Tirana, 2013, p. 252.
16 Jonas Staal, "To Make a World, Part I: Ultranationalism and the Art of the Stateless State", Ibid.

State (or, even, ultra-nationalism) the last remaining obstacle in achieving true internationalism?
I think that the exclusion of non-separatist political agents from Staal's parliament inscribes his endeavor in the direction of a conservative revolution: a reduction of internationalism to separatist regionalism. The only "coordination" achieved by the very contextual boundaries of this parliament is the coordination between a variety of struggles and a right-wing messianic impulse to redeem the lost communities of the past. In a sense, contemporary Greece is an example of the failure of such a vision. The articulation of an identity of resistance against E.U's conservative economic policies in terms of national liberationism gave birth to a sterile milieu of regressive political agencies with a grim future.

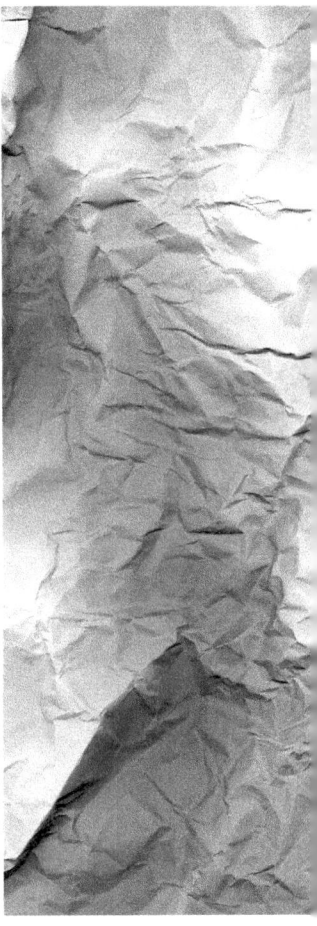

_ Kostis Stafylakis

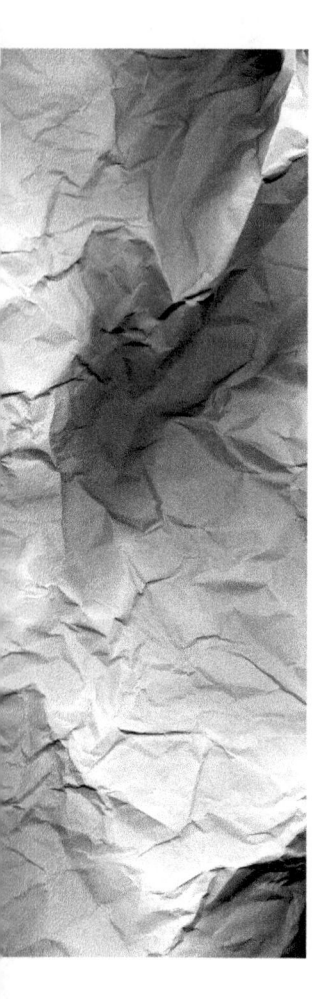

About this publication

Project Management: Heiko Schmid
Editors: Heiko Schmid & Kostis Stafylakis
Subeditor: Ian Rodney Wooldridge
Texts: Sofia Bempeza, Robin Klimecki, Elpida Rikou & Eleana Yalouri, Heiko Schmid, Kostis Stafylakis
Artistic Inputs (grey pages): Natasa Biza, Romy Rüegger, Vassilis Vlastaras, Zafos Xagoraris
Photos: Roland Regner (except p. 29-55 / grey pages)
Concept and Design: Roland Regner
Print: Tamvakos, Piliou 8, Peristeri
First Edition: 100 copies

Thanks to:
Beton7, Rania Kliari, Vasso Markou, Tamvakos Panagiotis

© The authors 2014
Minor Alterations of Legal Texts or other Regulations © Francoise Heitsch Gallery, Munich
ISBN 978-3-7386-0283-8
Printed and published by BoD - Books on Demand, Norderstedt

This publication appears within the framework of the exhibition „The Other Designs. Historical authenticity as artistic project".

Beton 7 Athens 30. October - 22. November 2014
Artists: Natasa Biza // Roland Regner // Romy Rüegger // Vassilis Vlastaras
Curators: Heiko Schmid & Kostis Staylakis

Supported by the "Dossier Internationales" and the "Department of Art & Media", Zurich University of Arts.

Z hdk
Zürcher Hochschule der Künste
Zurich University of the Arts